THE
ELOQUENT
LEADER

EXCLUSIVE, LIMITED-EDITION VERSION

The Eloquent Leader

———

———

CONTENTS

—

—

———

———

———

———

———

———

―――

―――

———

———

―――

―――

THE PREAMBLE

PRAISE FOR PETER'S WORK…

"A very tactical, practical, and engaging read packed with step-by-step strategies that are backed with compelling evidence."

"One of the best books on leadership I've ever read."

"Packed with unique and powerful paradigm-shifting advice on the most important key to successful leadership: effective communication."

"I highly recommend this book (and the whole set of crash courses which I'm steadily working through) for anyone who wants to empower their leadership."

"This book introduced me to brand new dimensions of leadership. Essential reading for any business managers who want to speak with major impact and influence."

"By far the best and most information-packed read on business communication I know of."

"If you would like to improve your professional image (as the author says), speak with more confidence and credibility, and learn how to do these things from an engaging and captivating book that keeps you hooked, this should be your next read."

"I highly recommend this book (and all this author's books) for anyone who works in any business field and wants to improve their communication."

"It teaches practical, step-by-step strategies that are easily applicable to so many everyday situations in professional life, like presentations, meetings, interviews, etc."

"The new How to Win Friends and Influence People."

"As someone who works in business management and as someone who has read a few books by this author, I can testify to the fact that CREDIBLE communication is a necessity for business success. I enjoyed this book because that's what it focuses on."

———

"While I'm fairly well-versed as a communicator, this book taught me so many advanced strategies I had no idea existed."

"As this book demonstrates, effective business communication goes much deeper than most people realize. Based on my experience, this book is a must-read because the following happens all the time: someone will speak, and while their idea is good, their presentation lacks credibility and it gets shot down."

"I need to talk to a lot of people in my career, and usually I need to influence them to do something. This book showed me plenty of strategies I haven't come across so far in my career, that are actionable, practical, and effective."

"If you find yourself in situations where you need to change peoples minds, convince them of the value of your product, experience, or ideas, or simply communicate with more clarity, this book will help you."

———

"If you liked 'How to Win Friends and Influence People' by Dale Carnegie, you'll like this book too."

"Having read a fair number of books on communication skills, business communication, and the like, I will tell you that the content you'll find in this one won't be found anywhere else."

"I think this book is a must-read for anyone who needs to interact with a lot of people in their career, not just those struggling with interpersonal communication."

"Need to give a presentation? This book will teach you how. Need to know how to change someone's mind? This book will teach you how. Want to know what mistakes to avoid making in professions conversations, business meetings, or any communication? This book has you covered."

"Loved it! Snappy and fast-paced writing that kept me engaged."

"Full of valuable information. Unlike many books of its kind, none of this information could be found online in blog posts for free. Even the basic information that is available elsewhere is taken to a whole new depth."

"Do you think your communication could be better? If you need to speak in meetings or give presentations at work, this book will help you turn those situations into opportunities to build support for yourself and your ideas. I recommend this for anyone who wants to do that."

"This was the best purchase I've ever made. Not just book purchase... purchase in general."

"I've been compelled to write this after only reaching page 68 in my first sit-down with the book. This is the sweet nectar of the communication gods delivered with fervor by the author."

—

"Amazing wealth of knowledge in a well-structured format. And if you're in sales of any kind - stop reading this review and buy already. Your commission stubs will thank you."

"The bonus video course and eBooks were a big plus for me. I recommend it for any leader / aspiring leader who wants to turn forgettable communication into language that people remember, take to heart, and act on."

"I am still reading along with other non-fiction books. It is a nice refresher course for me. Others will find it helpful to get a handle on how one speaks and listens!"

"Just like, 'What Color Is Your Parachute?' is an imperative book to read for networking techniques and life success, Peter's book is as well."

"Something severely lacking in today's world is effective verbal communication. In a world dominated by texting and emails, effective communication has fallen to the wayside. People have largely lost the ability to

—

———

communicate. As a college student and US Army veteran, communication is a vital aspect to success in life."

"Highly recommended for anyone who wants to communicate more effectively in a professional setting."

"Easy to read and understand."

"Here's what I learned from this book: exactly how to effectively communicate in business or a professional setting."

"If you need to speak in meetings, give presentations, persuade people in your career, or write to get people to take action, you need to know these methods."

"Amazing book, would recommend to anyone interested in learning more about communication!"

"I enjoyed this one because it is broadly applicable to all communication. I used to stutter constantly and struggle

———

with clearly communicating my ideas. This was really helpful because it gave me clear structures."

"Helped me clarify my communication and get people to listen."

"The author covers easy and simple techniques; the author seems to have lots of expertise. Very fun to read and fast paced."

"Having read a few books on this subject, I can tell you that I learned more in the first 30 pages of this book than in the entirety of most others."

"Such an amazing book. I never truly understood the art of effective speaking until I started reading this book! He covers the key points of communication and I would recommend this book to everybody because this will help people in a long run!"

———

"You can't succeed in your career without effective communication. And you can't master effective communication without this book."

"When someone asked me to give a conference about my life - the first part - I felt not only honored but also really appreciated. And this book helped me to prepare as if I were about to talk to the whole world, and this has no price."

"Peter's style and expertise of public speaking, debate, and general conversation is incredibly captivating. When you add in the understanding that he overcame a speech impediment to become the Massachusetts State Champion, it's all but certain you have something to learn from him."

"Peter's strategies are straightforward yet unconventional. I would guarantee this book can assist you with leveling up your public speaking abilities, leading to an overall boost in not only confidence but performance in your career, education, or entrepreneurial journey."

"Awesome read filled with tons of step by step techniques."

"I am much more confident speaking in front of an audience today than ever before I read this."

"I can actually use each and every one of the techniques in the book: they aren't abstract pieces of vague advice that do more to confuse/distract me than help me."

"The author eases the reader with an abundance of information at a level that anyone is able to comprehend. When reading the book, your time doesn't feel wasted or that the book drags on. It is full of useful tips and tricks and has helped me a ton with presentations and campaign speeches. Each section is straight to the point and has so much information that everyone could benefit by reading it."

"I was recommended this book by a friend and my speaking was completely transformed. The methods offered in the book are extremely practical and make it easy to follow."

"This book was amazing. It was clear, engaging, easy to read, and gave more than enough information and multiple approaches to truly help me become a better speaker. For the price, I got a wealth of information, and was well worth the money. The bonus content was also extremely helpful and put me over the edge on this purchase. Overall, a great book, that will truly help you become a better speaker. I have noticed a difference in my speaking, and you will too!"

"Soo helpful! I used it to overcome my excessive word vomit, and in a matter of weeks, my public speaking skills had clearly increased, even bringing one audience to their feet with applause after giving a forceful and relatable speech."

"I like how the broad concepts are explained first and then complex and specific techniques are explained later."

"Very concise and clean writing. Easy to grasp and quick to the point."

"Loved the short chapters. They held my attention for a long time. The writing is engaging and polished. I honestly expected to be inundated with a wave of cliche advice and useless truisms, and I was pleasantly surprised."

"The first 20 pages alone were worth the price I paid for the book. I recommend this book to anyone who needs to communicate effectively in their career. don't forget, when you purchase this book you also have access to the bonus content, including the video course."

"This book was very helpful to me. The techniques outlined in it proved easy to learn and easy to implement."

___

"I suggest this book to anyone who has presentation anxiety, has a career or job which requires lots of presentations, or wants to become a better public speaker. A lot of the methods I learned can be used in meetings or smaller talks."

"Very well written and highly insightful. As someone who struggles with anxiety in regards to public speaking, this book was able to help me curb that consistent fear."

"This is a self-help book that WILL make you a better speaker."

"Beats or rivals the public speaking education at Ivy League institutions that cost hundreds of thousands of dollars to attend."

"I find myself using these strategies and frameworks in my daily life."

"I feel like a stronger leader and better communicator."

___

DON'T BE FOOLED...

Don't let me fool you. Throughout this book, and in basically anything I ever wrote or recorded on the subjects of communication, persuasion, influence, and leadership (which are all really one subject), I present information through the lens of public speaking. Why? Because that's my background. That's how I got my start. My journey as a competitive public speaker is what led me on *this* journey – the journey of compiling the frameworks and strategies leaders need to communicate with influence. This background informs all my work and colors all my writing. But remember this: Whenever I describe a strategy through the lens of giving a public speech or presentation, it applies to virtually all professional communication.

Proposals...

Emails...

Pitches...

———

Interviews...

Meetings...

Informal (but high-stakes) conversations...

Whatever form of communication you can think of, it's all really one and the same when you strip away the superficial differences. It's all transmitting an idea from your mind into another mind (or millions of other minds). So if I say, hypothetically, "the problem-solution structure is a simple and compelling framework you can use to create a fast and psychologically irresistible persuasive punch in your speech," know that what I'm really saying is this: "The problem-solution structure is a simple and compelling framework you can use to create a fast and psychologically irresistible persuasive punch *in all communication, no matter its superficial form.*"

Moving on...

———

WANT TO LEAD?

Learn to speak.

The world's legendary leaders are also legendary communicators. They can take an idea existing in their minds, replicate it in other minds, and build a mass movement devoted to manifesting it. They can subtly compel others to think a certain way, act a certain way, and live a certain way. They can immediately earn trust, portray credibility, and achieve automatic authority.

They can argue well, present proposals well, and persuade well. They can instantly influence nearly anyone, in nearly any situation, to believe nearly anything. They can speak with complete confidence in themselves, their ideas, and their visions for the future. They are visionaries. They are those who ask not "why?" but "why *not?*" and inspire others to perform incredible feats, like putting a man on the moon, or defeating Nazi Germany.

They are empaths: They understand how others feel, and how to communicate to those feelings. They are powerful: They are deadly effective because they are severely well-equipped to reign in the only important battleground, the battleground of ideas. They win under the weight of the burdens buckling others. They are bold and brave, capable and competent, persuasive and powerful. They match good intentions with an ability to make a difference. Their presence is a gift to everyone around them.

And here's my question to you: Will you be one of them?

If your bad presentation kills your good ideas, it also kills your career. If your proposals fall flat, failing to inspire others, you miss opportunities daily. If your communication doesn't convey complete self-confidence, you might falter at a critical moment, undermine your professional image, and accidentally pull a premature hand-break on your career, grinding it to a frustrating halt and weakening your leadership.

———

Communication creates reality. And leaders shape our world. How? By communicating big ideas in big ways; by inspiring passion for a key proposal on a grand scale. Or on a miniscule scale. Big or small, grand or humble, a goal demands a team. Nobody succeeds alone. Nobody builds anything worth building without the contribution of other people and, sometimes, a lot of them. And nobody gets this contribution – a key to leadership – without effective communication.

That's why all leaders are highly effective communicators. That's why they play a role in shaping our world.

And here's my follow-up question: Do you want to claim your rightful stake in this ongoing project, this never-finished mission of building the world? Or do you want to cede it to someone else – someone with stronger communication, but weaker ideas? If you accept the challenge of changing our world, you'll need to develop many qualities. The most important? Effective communication.

———

MY PROMISE TO YOU…
Here's the truth.

Unlike many of my fellow nonfiction authors, I don't believe you need 592,431,965,172 anecdotes, examples, and stories to grasp a point.

I think you just need to hear the point.

I know you're busy. I know you need information, not stories. Tactics, not anecdotes. Proven methods based on infallible foundations, not advice drawn from a single distant memory (accompanied by 40 pages relaying of the memory…)

Chances are you have a lot going on. Chances are you have important things to do. And chances are, if this book wastes your time, it won't be as big a help as it could have been.

And to me, that would be tragic.

———

So, what's my promise to you? Brevity. You get what you need to get to go from communication that holds you back to communication that propels you forward.

Countless books on the subject of communication, particularly communication for leaders, don't offer what this book offers. (And I know this because I wrote half of them...)

And what does this book offer?

Everything you need.

Nothing you don't.

That's my promise to you.

Shall we begin? You decide.

———

THE TEN STEPS

A brief preview so you know how each step fits into the whole scheme.

Improve your structure. Structure is everything. Structure is make-or-break. What's a structure? A sequence of communication "steps" producing the desired result. What desired result? *Your* desired result. Whether it's proving a claim, overcoming objections, creating desire for a product, or supporting an idea, there's a proven, step-by-step process accomplishing it better than anything else. No structure? No success. And there are a few guidelines: Structures can be lengthened and shortened like an accordion. They will maintain their impact proportionally. Structures can be stacked, delivered one after the other as you see fit. And finally, structures can be nested. How? By using an entire structure to accomplish a step in another structure.

Improve your words. Your words have to work. They must be clean. They must be clear. They must compel. The problem? Most people speak with weak words, undermining themselves and their message. Why? Because they don't know how to improve their words. But you will.

Improve your message. Your structure organizes your words in a sequence. Your words carry your message. And some messages work. Others don't. The good part? We know what makes a message work and why some messages don't.

Improve your vocal tonalities. You have three languages. You have your word language, your vocal language, and your body language. Want people to listen when you speak? To trust you? To agree with your positions and enthusiastically support your proposals? You must speak to them with all three of your voices. A good structure filled with good words delivering a good message falls short if the voice speaking these things fails to captivate and compel. You'll know how to guarantee yours does.

―――

Improve your body language. How you stand. How you gesture. Your facial expression. The position of your body. Your posture. Your movements. Your micro-movements. Where your eyes look. Where your palms face. What do these have in common? They all *say* something without *saying* something. And if you don't take control of them, they still say something: Just the wrong thing; the thing hurting you instead of helping you.

Improve your appeal. What's appeal? Words with appeal create an irresistible psychological pull. And predictable, repeatable concepts create appeal. If you play upon them, your idea, message, product, proposal, or whatever your thing is, adopts the same irresistible and immensely powerful pull.

Improve your visuals. You probably need to use presentation software in your line of work. And you probably make the same exact mistakes 99% of people make with their slides. Don't. They undermine you and your message, boring people instead of engaging them.

―――

Improve your hook. If you get everything else right, but lack the attention of those you're speaking to, you might as well get everything else wrong. Why? Because no attention equals no communication. If your audience tunes out, you're sending something out there, but nobody is picking it up. You're speaking to thin air. But you can avoid this with a hook at your start (and whenever you need to grab attention).

Improve your eloquence. Want to master the secret strategies of supremely eloquent language? Language presidents and top CEOs pay armies of speech writers to create? And want to apply these strategies instantly, on the spot, with nearly no practice? It's easier than it sounds if you know the right frameworks.

Improve your mindset. What's the point? Why improve your mindset? Does it really make a difference? *"Do I have to?"* Depends: Do you want to prevent debilitating anxiety before high-stakes presentations? If so, you must improve your mindset. But it gets better: Improving your mindset enables you to quickly,

---

effortlessly, and naturally use the concrete strategies you learned in the previous nine steps. You'll find out how.

———

STEP ONE
IMPROVE YOUR STRUCTURE

1.1: PROBLEM, AGITATE, SOLUTION
What is it?

Present a problem your audience faces. Agitate the problem. Present your solution to the problem. It's that simple. "Your task will not be an easy one *(Problem)*. Your enemy is well trained, well equipped and battle-hardened. He will fight savagely *(Agitate)*. But this is the year 1944! Much has happened since the Nazi triumphs of 1940-41. The United Nations have inflicted upon the Germans great defeats, in open battle, man-to-man. Our air offensive has seriously reduced their strength in the air and their capacity to wage war on the ground. Our Home Fronts have given us an overwhelming superiority in weapons and munitions of war, and placed at our disposal great reserves of trained fighting men. The tide has turned! The free men of the world are marching together to Victory! *(Solution)*" – Dwight D. Eisenhower

Why does it work?

Would you ever buy medicine if you weren't sick? Of course not. In a sentence, this structure works because

---

solutions only make sense in the context of the problems they solve. By defining the problem – and by starting with the problem – the solution becomes drastically and dramatically more attractive when you present it. The solution suddenly makes sense. Its appeal and value become self-evident. And as a result, people want it.

How do you do it?

Ask yourself: What's the biggest problem my audience faces solved by my proposal? That takes care of the problem step. What emotions does it cause? How can I emphasize the problem? How can I make it seem more urgent, extreme, and important? How can I tie the external problem to internal problems (negative emotions)? These questions take care of the agitate step. Finally: What's my solution? How does it feel when they use it to solve the problem? How does it work? Why can they trust it? With that, you conclude the solution step and the structure. Simple, right? All you have to do is fill in the proven, step-by-step formula. It's both an easier and more effective way of communicating.

1.2: PAST, PRESENT, MEANS
What is it?

Present the problems of the past. Describe the improved present. Share the means with which the difficult past turned into the positive present. "The South Bend I grew up in was still recovering from economic disasters that played out before I was even born. Once in this city, we housed companies that helped power America into the 20th century. Think of the forces that built the building we're standing in now, and countless others like it now long gone. Think of the wealth created here. Think of the thousands of workers who came here every day, and the thousands of families they provided for. And think of what it must have been like in 1963 when the great Studebaker auto company collapsed and the shock brought this city to its knees. Buildings like this one fell quiet, and acres of land around us slowly became a rust-scape of industrial decline, collapsing factories everywhere. Houses, once full with life and love and hope, stood crumbling and vacant. For the next half-century it took heroic efforts just to keep our city running, while our population shrank, and young people like me grew up believing the only way to a good life was to get out. Many of us did. But then some of us came back. We wanted things to change around here. And when the national press called us a dying city at the beginning of this decade, we took it as a call to arms. I ran for mayor in 2011 knowing that nothing like Studebaker would ever come back – but believing that we would, our city would, if we had the courage to reimagine our future *(Past)*. And now, I can confidently say that South Bend is back. More people are moving into South Bend than we've seen in a generation. Thousands of new jobs have been added in our area, and billions in investment. There's a long way for us to go. Life here is far from perfect. But we've changed our trajectory, and shown a path forward for communities like ours *(Present)*. And that's why I'm here today. To tell a different story than 'Make America Great Again.' Because there is a myth being sold to industrial and rural communities: the myth that we can stop the clock and turn it back. It comes from people who think the only way to reach communities like ours is through resentment and nostalgia, selling an impossible promise of returning to a bygone era that was never as great as advertised to begin with. The problem is, they're telling us to look for greatness in all the wrong places. Because if there is one thing the city of South Bend has shown, it's that there is no such thing as an honest politics that revolves around the word 'again.' It's time to walk away from the politics of the past, and toward something totally different *(Means)*." – Pete Buttigieg

Why does it work?

By contrasting the problems of the past with the successes of the present, it builds suspense and desire for the *means*: For *how* the change happened. It also earns trust, building credibility for the plan by presenting an example of it working in the past.

How do you do it?

Ask yourself: What problems are people facing now? When did I (or someone else my audience can identify with) face these problems? How can I tell a story about this? This takes care of the present step. Next: What is life like for me now (or for your "character" – *South Bend* in Pete's case)? In what ways is it better? In what ways did the problems of the past evaporate, making way for an aspirational and attractive present? That covers the present step. Last: How did the change happen? What solution turned the problematic past into the successful present? And how can your audience replicate it?

1.3: DEMAND, OPPORTUNITY, SATISFACTION
What is it?

Present people's demand. Present the opportunity you're offering them to satisfy the demand. Present the need for action on their part to use the opportunity to satisfy the demand. "The American people have summoned the change we celebrate today. You have raised your voices in an unmistakable chorus. You have cast your votes in historic numbers *(Demand)*. And you have changed the face of Congress, the presidency and the political process itself *(Opportunity)*. Yes, you, my fellow Americans have forced the spring. Now, we must do the work the season demands *(Satisfaction)*." – Bill Clinton

___

Why does it work?

By highlighting the demand, this structure activates social proof: Our tendency to follow the crowd, wanting what it wants, doing what it does, avoiding what it avoids. It expresses how many people *wanted* the opportunity, and as a result, makes many more people *start* wanting it. This flows into the opportunity step, presenting an opportunity capable of satisfying the demand. Because of the demand step, the opportunity you're offering seems significantly more attractive. And the satisfaction step delivers the final persuasive punch, emphasizing the need for audience action; for them to start wielding the opportunity to satisfy the demand.

How do you do it?

Ask yourself: How have people displayed their demand for a change? What is the proof many people demanded it? This covers the demand step. Next: What is the opportunity? What did I create to satisfy this demand? How does it serve as an opportunity to satisfy the demand? Opportunity step complete. How can I call my audience to action, showing them the opportunity won't

___

work on its own to satisfy the demand, but that it calls for further action on their part? Satisfaction step done.

1.4: CHOICE, OPTION, OPTION
What is it?

Presenting a moment of choice. Presenting the option you propose. Presenting the inferior alternative. "You and I are told we must choose between a left or right *(Choice)*, but I suggest there is no such thing as a left or right. There is only an up or down. Up to man's age-old dream – the maximum of individual freedom consistent with order *(Option)* or down to the ant heap of totalitarianism *(Option)*. Regardless of their sincerity, their humanitarian motives, those who would sacrifice freedom for security have embarked on this downward path. Plutarch warned, 'The real destroyer of the liberties of the people is he who spreads among them bounties, donations and benefits.'" – Ronald Reagan

Why does it work?

By presenting a moment of choice – an impending decision – it grabs attention. Then, by presenting two

___

options (what you suggest and an alternative) and allowing the contrast between the two to take effect, it makes your proposal appear self-evidently superior. And human perception functions through contrasts and comparisons (more on this later). By presenting your superior idea next to the inferior alternative, you appeal to contrast and make your idea seem better than it would in isolation.

How do you do it?

Ask yourself: What impending moment of decision do we have? How can I present this incoming need to choose – this fork in the road – in a captivating way? Choice step done. For the next step: What is my proposal, acting as their first option? How can I portray it as self-evidently superior? Finally: What is the alternative to my proposal, and their second option (and "do nothing" can be an alternative to acting as you want)? How can I portray it as self-evidently inferior? How can I paint the contrasts between the options in a vivid and compelling way?

___

1.5: VICTIM, PERPETRATOR, BENEVOLENCE
What is it?

Presenting how your audience members are victims of a breach in justice. Presenting the perpetrator who breached justice against them. Presenting yourself, your product, your offering, your proposal, or your group as the benevolent force for good, which can heal the victim, punish the perpetrator, and restore justice. This structure can occur in any order. "Well, I don't think they really do like the economy. Go back and talk to the old neighbors in the middle-class neighborhoods you grew up in. The middle class is getting killed. The middle class is getting crushed and the working class has no way up as a consequence of that. You have, for example, farmers in the Midwest, 40 percent of them could pay, couldn't pay their bills last year. You have most Americans, if they've received the bill for 400 dollars or more, they'd have to sell something or borrow the money. The middle class is not, is behind the eight ball *(Victims)*. We have to make sure that they have an even shot. We have to eliminate significant number of these god-awful tax cuts that were given to the very wealthy.

We have to invest in education. We have to invest in healthcare. We have to invest in those things that make a difference in the lives of middle-class people so they can maintain their standard of living *(Benevolence)*. That's not being done, and the idea that we're growing, we're not growing. The wealthy, very wealthy are growing. Ordinary people are not growing. They are not happy with where they are, and that's why we must change this presidency now *(Perpetrators)*." – Joe Biden

Why does it work?

It's a story of a benevolent source of goodness (you, your product, your organization, etc.) protecting victims (your audience) from a perpetrator (whoever is causing the problems for the audience). It works for myriad reasons, activating a host of features of human psychology in the same direction all at once: Our desire for justice, the appeal of victimhood, the pleasure of punishing perpetrators and enemies, the intuitive appeal of an archetype-driven narrative, the inherent and inalienable appeal of moral values, and countless others.

How do you do it?

First: What problems plague your audience? Why are they victims? And why do the problems represent more than mere inconveniences? Why do they represent deep fractures in the fabric of morality? Second: How are you going to heal them, fixing the problems? How are you going to act as a benevolent force for good? How are you going to beat back and punish the perpetrators? Third: Who are the perpetrators? The ones who caused the victim's problems, and the ones you bring to justice?

1.6: INVITATION, STORY, EPIPHANY
What is it?

Present your audience with an invitation into a story that first gave you the core persuasive epiphany you want them to have now. Present the story. Present the epiphany. "Not too long ago, two friends of mine were talking to a Cuban refugee, a businessman who had escaped from Castro, and in the midst of his story one of my friends turned to the other and said *(Invitation)*, "We don't know how lucky we are." And the Cuban stopped and said, "How lucky you are? I had someplace to escape to." *(Story)* And in that sentence he told us the entire story. If we lose freedom here, there's no place to escape to. This is the last stand on Earth *(Epiphany)*." – Ronald Reagan

Why does it work?

Stories are inherently, inalienably, intrinsically and irresistibly influential constructions. Stories are as old as language itself. They appeal to human intuition. And humans love listening to them. So when you invite them into a story, they come along, giving you undivided attention. And here's the key: The best way to get people to believe something is to tell them a story which will help them come to the conclusion themselves. Telling the story that gave you the epiphany will replicate the epiphany in their minds. And of course, enumerating the epiphany guarantees everyone is on the same page.

How do you do it?

First: How can you signal a story? How can you invite them into a narrative? What's the context? The setup? How can you hook them? Who are the main characters, what are the main components, and what are the other key elements? Second: What's the story? How can you engineer it to recreate the epiphany the events first gave you? Third: In case anyone missed it or isn't sure, what is the epiphany?

1.7: BEFORE, AFTER, BRIDGE
What is it?

This is a modified version of the Past, Present, Means structure. While the Past, Present, Means structure tells the story of someone or something going from a bad past to a good present, and then reveals how, the Before, After, Bridge structure says this: "Here's what you're struggling with *now*. This is the pain you feel *now*. These are the shortcomings of the *current moment (Before)*. But it doesn't have to be that way. You can experience this incredible life. You can feel these positive emotions. Your future can be abundant in the exact ways the present is lacking *(After)*. You can make the shift by taking this action *(Bridge)*."

—

Why does it work?

It works by appealing to emotion, first echoing the negative emotions of the present and contrasting them with the positive emotions possible in the future. This contrast, like the one in the Choice, Option, Option structure, makes both items seem more vivid and compelling. And it works because this emotional rollercoaster paints an aspirational vision for the future, creating immense desire for the action that can bridge the lacking present to the abundant future. Emotion is the gateway to influence. And emotion creates action where logic and facts fail to inspire any. Of course, use both emotion and logic for the best results. Lastly, people only act for two reasons. This structure activates both. The two reasons? To move away from pain and towards pleasure; away from the pain of the present and towards the pleasure possible in the future.

How do you do it?

First: What pain-points do your audience members face? What can you assume about the emotional pain they feel? How can you portray empathy and understanding?

—

How can you call out clear and compelling problems in the present? Second: How can you cast an aspirational vision of the future? How will this potential future be better than the present? How can you sprinkle proof throughout, to make this seem like a real possibility? Third: What's the bridge, taking them from where they don't want to be (but where they are) to where they want to go? And why should they trust it? What's the proof it won't crumble under their feet?

1.8: PACING, STORY, LEADING
What is it?

Persuasion is, in part, getting people to stop believing what they believe and start believing what you believe. Pacing is echoing the sentiments of your audience members. Leading is replacing those sentiments with your sentiments. In short: Let's say your audience's belief is that "X is Y." Let's say your belief, what you want them to adopt, is "X is Z." (Y and Z, by the way, don't have to be opposites). Pacing is saying "X is Y." Leading is saying "X is Z." Pacing and leading is slowly sliding from "X is Y" to "X is Z." So the structure goes

———

something like this: "I agree. X is Y, for these reasons *(Pacing)*. I remember something that changed my perspective a little. Here's the story that initially made me realize X is Z *(Story)*. X is Z *(Leading)*."

Why does it work?

Just like the Invitation, Story, Epiphany structure, it subtly embeds the core epiphany you want your audience to have in the facade of a story, sneakily getting them to realize the epiphany themselves. This is much more effective than hammering it into their heads. And it works because it avoids triggering the endowment effect and reactance. The endowment effect is the irrational and objectively non-existent value people add to the true value of what they consider theirs. It applies to beliefs too: People endow their own beliefs with added value. When you threaten their beliefs, you threaten something they find immensely valuable. Good luck. And reactance is the psychological resistance humans have to someone trying to compel us to do or believe something (which is why all the methods in this book try to inspire action from within, not force it from

———

---

without). When you say "you're wrong," people jump behind their cognitive defenses. Why? Because people avoid psychological pain. Cognitive dissonance, perceiving a contradiction between reality and our beliefs about reality, is painful. And if you're saying "you're wrong" to them, you cause cognitive dissonance. They pull out their disconfirmation guns, ready to say "no, I'm not!" becoming further entrenched in their positions than they were before. Pacing – meeting them where *they* are – before telling a story that slowly slides into leading – taking them where *you* want to go – avoids all these pitfalls, and the dynamic duo of defeat that is the endowment effect and reactance. When you pace and lead, they feel validated, so they are more likely to validate your positions, accepting them with enthusiasm. I keep hearing communication thought leaders saying "A confused mind always says no." Correct. But what's even more important to understand? *A threatened mind always says "hell no, you're wrong, I'm right, and leave me alone."*

―――

How do you do it?

Pacing: How can you echo where your audience is in a way that seems genuine and real? Story: What's the story that gave you the epiphany moving you from where they are to where you currently are? Leading: How can you reinforce this epiphany in your audience's minds?

1.9: CLAIM, EVEN IF, CHAIN
What is it?

Making a claim about how something works or the benefits it offers, predicting the main objections, concerns, or doubts people will have, and overcoming them by saying it works even if [insert objection], chaining these statements together for as many objections as you want. "Doing this offers you these tremendous benefits *(Claim)*, even if *(Even if)* you have this objection… Even if you… Even if you… Even if you… Even if you… Even if you… *(Chain)*."

Why does it work?

People can be skeptical. Our minds frequently serve us objections upon hearing a claim or promise. "This helps

―――

businesses segment their email lists." *Oh yeah? Well what if we already had it poorly segmented by a cheap software? I bet it doesn't work then.* Something like that. People need certainty before acting. And if they have lingering objections, you need to address them to get certainty and action.

How do you do it?

Claim: What's your main benefit promise? Even if: What's the biggest common objection? Chain: The third? Fourth? Fifth? So on and so forth.

1.10: AUTHORITY-CLAIM, QUANT-QUAL, CLAIM
What is it?

Making a claim linked to your authority on the subject, providing quantitative evidence (statistics and other numerical evidence) for the claim, providing qualitative evidence for the claim (anecdotes, stories, and examples), and then restating the claim. "Based on seven years working on this type of problem, it's clear that what's going on is *(Authority-Claim)...* The proof? According to this research center, X% of... *(Quantitative*

———

evidence). Just last year, I remember seeing… *(Qualitative evidence).* This all suggests… *(Claim).*"

Why does it work?

About 2,400 years ago Aristotle identified the three core elements of persuasion: Ethos, the credibility of the speaker; Pathos, the emotional appeal of the persuasive message; Logos, the logical appeal of the persuasive message. 2,400 years later, this rhetorical triad has been reconfirmed and reconfirmed over and over again. And why does this structure work? Because it achieves all three of these prerequisites to persuasion. The authority-claim presents Ethos, the quantitative evidence appeals to logic, and the qualitative evidence appeals to emotion.

How do you do it?

Authority-claim: What's your authority on the subject? How can you present it in an honest, genuine way that is impressive without sounding like you're bragging? And based on this authority, what claim do you make? Quant-qual: What's the quantitative proof for your claim? Are the sources reputable? What's the qualitative proof for

———

---

your claim? How can you make this anecdote, story, or example emotionally compelling? Claim: How can you restate your claim – now that you've proven it through both emotional and logical pathways and established your authority – in an eloquent, hard-hitting way?

STEP TWO
IMPROVE YOUR WORDS

———

2.1: USE VARIED SENTENCE LENGTH

What is it?

Speaking in sentences with varied length, structure, and syntax: "That's why we do this. That's what politics can be. That's why elections matter. It's not small, it's big. It's important. Democracy in a nation of 300 million can be noisy and messy and complicated. We have our own opinions. Each of us has deeply held beliefs. And when we go through tough times, when we make big decisions as a country, it necessarily stirs passions, stirs up controversy. That won't change after tonight. And it shouldn't. These arguments we have are a mark of our liberty, and we can never forget that as we speak, people in distant nations are risking their lives right now just for a chance to argue about the issues that matter – the chance to cast their ballots like we did today." – Barack Obama

Why does it work?

Humans are pattern-recognizing creatures. And when you speak, you want to control attention. We give our attention to a pattern when we first perceive it developing. Then if it continues, it *habituates*, receding out of perception and losing our attention. And then that which *breaks* the pattern grabs our attention. Speaking sentences of the same length and with the same syntax and structure develops into a boring monotone pattern people can't stand listening to. Varied sentences make it interesting. Captivating. Engaging.

How do you do it?

Did you just deliver a long sentence? A sentence with complex syntax? With frequent flourishes? And a sentence that took on a lot, trying to impart, in one sentence, a big and complex chunk of meaning? Deliver a short one. Maybe a few short ones. But then change it up again. A medium one. Then a long one. Then a few short ones again. Pay attention to the captivating cadence of Obama's language in the example on the previous page, and you'll get an intuitive sense of how to create it yourself by varying sentence length.

2.2: USE TRANSITIONS

What is it?

Using language specifically designed to connect what you just said to what you're about to say. "At the same time... First, we have to talk about... On the other hand, when you look at... This is similar to... However... On the contrary... Despite this... But the essential idea is... Let's return to the idea of... Primarily... Thus... As a result... Hence... In addition... Moreover... For example..."

Why does it work?

If you grabbed attention, it's yours to lose. And you lose it by confusing people. Well: Transitioning from one idea to another idea without signaling the transition with your words confuses people. You have to answer the question: "How does this connect to what I just said?" Doing this ensures you keep audience attention without letting some of it leak away because people got confused by the incoherency of your transition-less communication.

___

How do you do it?

Ask yourself: "How does what I'm about to say connect to what I just said?" Then tell them. If this seems impractical in a fast-paced moment-by-moment communication situation, remember: Simply being aware of these concepts, and having them top of mind, makes it much more likely that you'll use them off-the-cuff.

2.3: USE MICRO-HOOKS

What is it?

Transitions in the form of short rhetorical questions: "Why does this happen? How? The result?" are some examples.

Why does it work?

It arouses curiosity. And it does so in as little as one word. Why? Because it frames a question. It's that simple. Questions captivate our attention. Humans love answers. And when we hear a question, we instinctively want the answer.

___

___

How do you do it?

State the question what you're about to say is going to answer. Do so in as few words as possible.

2.4: USE PATTERN-INTERRUPTS
What is it?

Elements of language designed to break away from patterns established by the preceding language.

Why does it work?

Patterns grab our attention at two points: When we first see them forming, and when we see them broken. And they lose our attention in between: When they continue for too long, they recede out of our perception. Pattern-interrupts avoid this, breaking them before they inevitably bore listeners.

How do you do it?

Ask yourself: "What patterns are my words forming?" Break them. Pay attention to word-choice. Syntax. Sentence length. Pay attention to everything. Break patterns offering no rhetorical effect.

___

—

2.5: USE SHORT, DIRECT, SIMPLE SENTENCES
What is it?

It's self-explanatory. Use short sentences. Focused sentences. Tight sentences. Sentences conveying only one idea. And a simple idea. An idea presented in its simplest form. Nothing unnecessary. Nothing useless.

Why does it work?

The human mind is designed to avoid expending mental calories unnecessarily. Our minds are designed to only pay attention to what helps us survive and thrive. And if listening to you has a high cognitive load, the mind is designed, by evolution, to tune out and save energy. Short, direct, simple sentences avoid this by acting as a mental "break." A moment of relief. Relaxation. Ease. The release of cognitive pressure. The escape of mental tension coming from preceding complexity. As such, they control attention. Or, rather, they guarantee you keep it, instead of losing it by *selling your information at too high a price of attention.*

—

___

How do you do it?

One-word sentences. Sentences in the form, "X [verbs] Y." Just three words. And sequences of such sentences for extended breaks.

2.6: USE ACTION-ORIENTED LANGUAGE
What is it?

Verb-saturated language describing what things *do* to other things, not what things *are*. "We are the keepers of this legacy. *Guided* by these principles once more we can *meet* those new threats that *demand* even greater effort, even greater cooperation and understanding between nations. We will begin to responsibly *leave* Iraq to its people and *forge* a hard-earned peace in Afghanistan. With old friends and former foes, we'll *work* tirelessly to *lessen* the nuclear threat, and *roll back* the specter of a warming planet." – Barack Obama

Why does it work?

Such language is scientifically proven to be more easily interpreted by the human mind. Don't forget this

___

---

essential mantra: *Convey information how the human mind is wired to receive information.*

How do you do it?

Use verbs. Tell us what it *does*. Not what it *is*. And the format "X [verb]s Y" produces action-oriented language as well as short, punchy sentences.

2.7: USE NATURAL LANGUAGE
What is it?

Speaking with the words that first appeared in your mind as the way to phrase an idea.

Why does it work?

The way an idea first appeared to you is often the most intuitive way of conveying it. It's not a hard-and-fast rule, but often the case.

How do you do it?

Don't rephrase things in your mind. Just lift your inhibitions and speak. Let it flow out of you. Trust yourself, and how ideas first crystallize in your mind.

2.8: USE INCLUSIVE PRONOUNS

What is it?

Using pronouns like "we, us, ours" that include the audience in the message instead of exclusive pronouns like "you" or "I." An example? "What I want you to understand is, the national debt is not the only cause of that. It is because America has not invested in its people; it is because *we* have not grown; it is because *we've* had twelve years of trickle-down economics. *We've* gone from first to twelfth in the world in wages, *we've* had four years when *we* produced no private sector jobs, most people are working harder for less money than they were making ten years ago. It is because *we* are in the grip of a failed economic theory. And this decision you're about to make better be about what kind of economic theory you want; not just people saying I wanna go fix it, but what are *we* going to do! What I think *we* have to do is invest in American jobs, American education, control American healthcare costs, and bring the American people together again." – Bill Clinton

---

Why does it work?

They put you and the audience on the same "team," subtly forming a psychological coalition: A tribe. They subtly implicate you as the spokesperson for this team. And they include your audience in your message, making them feel your empathy and drawing them into your communication.

How do you do it?

Not every "you" can be replaced by a "we." But for those that can be, do it.

2.9: AVOID PARANTHETICALS

What is it?

Parentheticals are attempts to interject an idea in the flow of your sentence in such a way that it would be signaled by parenthesis in writing. For example: "A sentence like this one, one that has twists and turns – even without big words – and a sentence which extends itself (and includes side-thoughts and related anecdotes in parenthesis) but doesn't concisely center on one idea, possibly including examples of many different ideas

---

under the roof of one sentence, though not tying them back to one – or perhaps two (but not three) – major thematic element or, in the case of more examples, elements plural, won't kill your writing (only coming close) but will kill (probably) your speaking."

Why does it work?

Why avoid parentheticals? They blur the clarity of your speech. Confused minds don't listen.

How do you do it?

They happen because you get an idea of what to say as you're delivering a sentence devoted to saying something else, and you deviate from that original purpose and try to stuff in the idea you just got. How do you avoid it? By catching yourself in the process before you try to stuff in the new idea, and pushing it back to a new sentence.

2.10: AVOID TANGENTS
What is it?

A tangent is an idea not connected to the original purpose of a sentence. Here's a sentence with no

---

tangent: "Denmark is not a good economic model for the United States because it is $1/60^{th}$ of the size." Here's a sentence with a tangent that loops back around into the original sentence: "Denmark is not a good economic model for the United States because – by the way, it has its own set of problems that we shouldn't be praising so highly – not to mention, though, that it is $1/60^{th}$ of the size." Here's a sentence with a tangent that concludes without looping back into the original sentence: "Denmark is not a good economic model for the United States because – by the way, it has its own set of problems that we shouldn't be praising so highly as virtually every single nation does that we seem to ignore when using it as a praiseworthy economy to replicate." And a sentence with tangents off of tangents: "Denmark is not a good economic model for the United States because – by the way, it has its own set of problems that we shouldn't be praising so highly as virtually every single nation does that we seem to ignore when using it as a praiseworthy economy to replicate, which is no different than the United States, not to mention their nonexistent need to protect half of Europe with their

---

military, like we do, which is why we can't have the social services they have."

Why does it work?

What do confused minds not do? Listen. And tangents confuse like nothing else.

How do you do it?

Much like parentheticals, you avoid tangents by catching yourself in the process *before* you try to stuff in the new idea, pushing it back to a new sentence.

STEP THREE
IMPROVE YOUR MESSAGE

___

3.1: PRESENT AN ASPIRATIONAL FUTURE
What is it?

Tying the attainment of an aspirational future to your message. "Your imagination, your initiative, and your indignation will determine whether we build a society where *progress is the servant of our needs*, or a society where old values and new visions are buried under unbridled growth. For in your time we have the opportunity to move not only toward the rich society and the powerful society, but *upward to the Great Society*. The Great Society rests on *abundance and liberty for all*. It demands *an end to poverty and racial injustice*, to which we are totally committed in our time. But that is just the beginning. The Great Society is a place *where every child can find knowledge to enrich his mind and to enlarge his talents*. It is a place where *leisure is a welcome chance to build and reflect, not a feared cause of boredom and restlessness*. It is a place where *the city of man serves not only the needs of the body and the demands of commerce but the desire for beauty and the hunger for community*. It is a place where *man can renew contact with nature*. It is a place which *honors creation for its own sake* and for what it adds to the understanding of the race. It is a

___

place where *men are more concerned with the quality of their goals than the quantity of their goods.* But most of all, the Great Society is not a safe harbor, a resting place, a final objective, a finished work. It is a challenge constantly renewed, beckoning us toward a destiny *where the meaning of our lives matches the marvelous products of our labor."* – Lyndon Johnson

Why does it work?

Aspirational persuasion is one of the most effective methods for inspiring people to take action. People only act in the name of preventing the future from getting worse (moving away from pain) or turning the future into something better (moving towards pleasure). Why? Because hundreds of thousands – if not millions upon millions – of years of evolution buried this duality in our minds.

How do you do it?

Tell them what they have to gain. Cast a vision of a better future. Portray the potential improvement, and the shortcomings of the present the future can overcome.

Tap into their deepest desires, painting a vision of a future in which they are abundantly satisfied. Give them hope.

3.2: PRESENT CONTRASTS
What is it?

Emphasizing a core persuasive epiphany through contrasts. "So, as we begin, let us take inventory. *We are a nation that has a government – not the other way around.* And this makes us special among the nations of the Earth. Our Government has no power except that granted it by the people. It is time to check and reverse the growth of government which shows signs of having grown beyond the consent of the governed. It is my intention to curb the size and influence of the Federal establishment and to demand recognition of the distinction between the powers granted to the Federal Government and those reserved to the States or to the people. *All of us need to be reminded that the Federal Government did not create the States; the States created the Federal Government.* Now, so there will be no misunderstanding, it is not my intention to do away with government. It is, rather, to make it work-*work*

―――

with us, not over us; to stand by our side, not ride on our back.
Government can and must provide opportunity, not smother it;
foster productivity, not stifle it." – Ronald Reagan

Why does it work?

Human perception is based on contrasts. Human
perception is based on comparisons. And contrasts, as a
result, influence us to a tremendous degree. We can't
judge an item in isolation. We need other items to which
we can compare it. And the more these items differ, the
more the unique characteristics of the item we are
evaluating announce themselves. They grow vivid.
Compelling. Powerful. By presenting a message
dominated by contrasting ideas, the core persuasive
epiphany you want to create in your audience becomes
self-evident.

How do you do it?

Talk about opposing ideas. Don't just talk about your
position. Talk about alternatives. And talk about why
they are inferior. Why yours is the best. Why the others
are lacking, if not fundamentally flawed. Talk about two

―――

different possible futures: One aspirational, and one of failure. Tell people what your idea is not. Tell people the intellectual status quo against which you rebel. Let the contrasts do the work for you, giving your words immense persuasive punch.

3.3: PRESENT A NEW PARADIGM
What is it?

The most attractive ideas are not incrementally better versions of old ideas, but revolutionary paradigms. Henry Ford once said that, if he asked, people would have said they wanted faster horses, not cars. Faster horses are incremental improvements. Cars are a new paradigm altogether. "Because there is a myth being sold to industrial and rural communities: the myth that we can stop the clock and turn it back. It comes from people who think the only way to reach communities like ours is through resentment and nostalgia, selling an impossible promise of returning to a bygone era that was never as great as advertised to begin with. The problem is, they're telling us to look for greatness in all the wrong places. Because if there is one thing the city of South

Bend has shown, it's that *there is no such thing as an honest politics that revolves around the word 'again.' It's time to walk away from the politics of the past, and toward something totally different.*" – Pete Buttigieg

Why does it work?

People find new paradigms innately exciting. They find them worthy. And they act in the name of actualizing them, simply due to the desire and hope the "shiny new thing" stokes.

How do you do it?

The first step is coming up with a new paradigm in the first place. And how to do so is beyond the scope of this book. The second step is presenting it. How? In a way emphasizing the novelty of the new approach. And by throwing stones at the old paradigm, calling out its deficiencies and failures, before presenting the new one you are offering.

3.4: PRESENT AN INNATE "WHY"
What is it?

Diving down to the deep reasons to do something. Appealing to the innate drives fulfilled by the action you propose. Diving beyond the superficial desires attached to your proposal, down to the deeply human reasons to want it on a deeply irresistible level. "We must provide for our nation the way a family *provides for its children*. Our Founders saw themselves in the light of posterity. We can do no less. Anyone who has ever watched a child's eyes wander into sleep knows what posterity is. Posterity is the world to come; the world for whom we hold our ideals, from whom we have borrowed our planet, and to whom we bear sacred responsibility. We must do what America does best: offer more opportunity to all and demand responsibility from all." – Bill Clinton

Why does it work?

The deeper the "why," the greater the persuasive pull. It's that simple.

How do you do it?

Now: Invoking a desire, once you identified it, isn't the hard part. What is, then? *Figuring out the deep desires at play in the first place.* But there's a simple algorithm for uncovering them. It's called the "why stack." How does it work? First, answer this question: "Why should people want to take this action? How will they specifically benefit?" Then answer this one: "Why should they want that benefit?" Then ask, of the answer to *that* question, "Why should they want *that* benefit?" Continue until you hit on a desire inherently, inalienably, and intrinsically worthwhile: Something you can't seem to move beyond. A desire for which the only answer to "why do we want it?" is "because we do."

3.5: PRESENT A STORY
What is it?

Embedding your core message in a story that represents the main idea. "Tonight is a particular honor for me because – let's face it – my presence on this stage is pretty unlikely. My father was a foreign student, born and raised in a small village in Kenya. He grew up

---

herding goats, went to school in a tin-roof shack. His father – my grandfather – was a cook, a domestic servant to the British. But my grandfather had larger dreams for his son. Through hard work and perseverance my father got a scholarship to study in a magical place, America, that shone as a beacon of freedom and opportunity to so many who had come before. While studying here, my father met my mother. She was born in a town on the other side of the world, in Kansas. Her father worked on oil rigs and farms through most of the Depression. The day after Pearl Harbor my grandfather signed up for duty; joined Patton's army, marched across Europe. Back home, my grandmother raised their baby and went to work on a bomber assembly line. After the war, they studied on the G.I. Bill, bought a house through F.H.A., and later moved west all the way to Hawaii in search of opportunity. And they, too, had big dreams for their daughter. A common dream, born of two continents. My parents shared not only an improbable love, they shared an abiding faith in the possibilities of this nation. They would give me an African name, Barack, or 'blessed,' believing that in a tolerant America your name is no barrier to success. They imagined me going to the best schools in the land, even though they weren't rich, because in a generous America you don't have to be rich to achieve your potential. They are both passed away now. And yet, I know that, on this night, they look down on me with great pride. I stand here today, grateful for the diversity of my heritage, aware that my parents' dreams live on in my two precious daughters. I stand here knowing that my story is part of the larger American story, that I owe a debt to all of those who came before me, and that, in no other country on earth, is my story even possible." – Barack Obama

Why does it work?

Stories are inherently captivating. Stories are tools for passing down meaning over thousands of years. Stories are irresistibly appealing to the human psychology. They appeal to hundreds of our cognitive biases, and a proclivity to listen to stories is very likely coded in our genes. Remember a core mantra of this book: Present information how the human mind is wired (by evolution) to receive it. Stories fall under the mandate of this mantra better than nearly anything else.

How do you do it?

Stories come in various shapes and sizes. But here's a compelling and simple mold: Who is your character? What does he want? Why does he want this? What are the obstacles, problems, villains, or barriers standing in his way? Why is what he wants good, and the alternate reality represented by the obstacles, problems, villains, or barriers not only not good, but a fundamentally immoral way of arranging the world? How does the character – the hero – go about moving the world from what it is to what he wants it to be? What does he learn, and how does he grow in the process? How does this lead to a transformation and rebirth, turning the character into a different, improved version of his old self? And here's some other advice: Keep it simple. Try to evoke bigger themes and universal ideals in the story: Adventure, opportunity, challenge, virtue, morality, rebirth, etc. Focus the story on one character. Make him or her a likeable character: Someone the audience can

———

identify with. Be specific. Focus on concrete details. Show, don't tell: Paint scenes representing the idea you want to convey instead of stating it flatly.

3.6: PRESENT A PLAN
What is it?

Presenting a concrete plan through which your message can become reality. "So I want to talk to you today about *three places where we begin to build the Great Society – in our cities, in our countryside, and in our classrooms.* Many of you will live to see the day, perhaps 50 years from now, when there will be 400 million Americans – four-fifths of them in urban areas. In the remainder of this century urban population will double, city land will double, and *we will have to build homes, highways, and facilities equal to all those built since this country was first settled. So in the next 40 years we must re-build the entire urban United States.* Aristotle said: "Men come together in cities in order to live, but they remain together in order to live the good life." It is harder and harder to live the good life in American cities today. The catalog of ills is long: there is the decay of the centers and the despoiling of the suburbs. There is not enough

———

---

housing for our people or transportation for our traffic. Open land is vanishing and old landmarks are violated. Worst of all expansion is eroding the precious and time-honored values of community with neighbors and communion with nature. The loss of these values breeds loneliness and boredom and indifference. Our society will never be great until our cities are great. *Today the frontier of imagination and innovation is inside those cities and not beyond their borders. New experiments are already going on.* It will be the task of your generation to make the American city a place where future generations will come, not only to live but to live the good life. I understand that if I stayed here tonight I would see that Michigan students are really doing their best to live the good life. This is the place where the Peace Corps was started. It is inspiring to see how all of you, while you are in this country, are trying so hard to live at the level of the people. A second place where we begin to build the Great Society is in our countryside…" – Lyndon Johnson

---

Why does it work?

People act to prevent pain or produce pleasure. But they have to first predict whether an action will produce the promised pleasure or prevent the foreshadowed pain. And in doing so, they adjust what you promised with how much they trust you and your proposed action. Got no trust? You can promise all the benefits in the world. You can promise all the pleasure and promise all the escape from pain. It won't matter. The predicted or perceived benefit will be zero. And here's the key: Presenting a plan ("*how* will we get it?") validates your benefits ("*what* will we get?"), raising trust and ensuring people perceive your benefits as worthy of action (because they believe in them).

How do you do it?

Answer these questions: How will we do it? How will we get these benefits? Why is this plan full-proof and nearly guaranteed to work? Upon what evidence is it based? How are we mitigating risk? How difficult is this plan? Why do we know this plan will work? When would this

---

plan have worked in a similar situation, were it implemented?

3.7: PRESENT YOURSELF AS A GUIDE
What is it?

Presenting your audience as the "heroes" in the story, not yourself. Presenting yourself as the "guide" who helps the heroes on their journey.

Why does it work?

Remember: Present information how the human mind is wired to receive it. Here's a secret: We all see ourselves as the heroes in our own stories, with everyone else acting as ancillary characters. Let's call this the "hero lens." Appealing to this hero lens, grafting yourself into the story the audience members – the heroes – are already telling themselves, and doing so as the guide, is an immensely psychologically intuitive message. As such, it persuades. It influences. It builds rapport and reciprocity, earning trust and laying the foundations for effective communication and a meaningful connection between you and your audience.

How do you do it?

First, position your audience as the hero. Remember the story mold from the previous step? Apply that mold with the audience in the role of the hero. When you get to the step in which they need to overcome the obstacle and turn the world from what it is to what they want it to be, position yourself as the guide who can help them do just that; a guide proposing a particular action.

3.8: PRESENT A MORAL NARRATIVE
What is it?

Presenting a persuasive messaged tied to a narrative about what is right and wrong. "This is one of those rare moments between whole eras in the life of our nation. I was born in another such moment, in the early 1980s, when a half-century of New Deal liberalism gave way to forty years of Reagan supply-side conservatism that created the terms for how Democrats as well as Republicans made policy. And that era, too, is now over. If America today feels like a confusing place to be, it's because we're on one of those blank pages in between chapters. Change is coming, ready or not. The question

---

of our time is whether families and workers will be defeated by the changes beneath us or whether we will master them and make them work toward a better everyday life for us all. Such a moment calls for hopeful and audacious voices from communities like ours. And yes, it calls for a new generation of leadership. The principles that will guide my campaign are simple enough to fit on a bumper sticker: freedom, security, and democracy." – Pete Buttigieg

Why does it work?

It appeals to drives and desires embedded in humans by tens of thousands of years of cultural evolution: Drives and desires centered around answering the inherent ethical questions of *"What is right? Wrong? Good? Bad?"*

How do you do it?

Why is what you're proposing the right thing to do? Why does it redress a moral wrongdoing? On what basic moral assumptions is your proposed action based? And what moral principles suggest your proposed action as

---

the right thing to do? How is the problem your proposed action solves a fundamental moral breach?

3.9: PRESENT A UNIFYING THEME
What is it?

Seeing your subject through a distinct lens – or theme – which unifies the entire message: "This ceremony is held in the *depth of winter*. But, by the words we speak and the faces we show the world, we force *the spring*. *A spring* reborn in the world's oldest democracy, that brings forth the vision and courage to reinvent America *(the start of a very long speech)*. [...] The American people have summoned the change we celebrate today. You have raised your voices in an unmistakable chorus. You have cast your votes in historic numbers. And you have changed the face of Congress, the presidency and the political process itself. Yes, you, my fellow Americans have *forced the spring*. Now, we must do the work the *season* demands *(the end of a very long speech)*." – Bill Clinton

Why does it work?

Theme-subject synergy just *works*. It evokes powerful and visceral emotions. It leaves people in agape wonder. What's theme-subject synergy? Presenting your subject through the lens of a theme which is both unique and perfectly fitting. It also acts as a memory anchor. Memory quickly recalls the simple theme. And once memory hits upon the simple theme, it takes the logical next step to the subject. And then it identifies how theme and subject fit together. And then it takes the next "memory step," and the next, until the message itself is fully recalled. More on this process later.

How do you do it?

Apply the Subject, Lens, Metaphor framework. Clinton's *subject* was America. He viewed America through the theme, or *lens*, of change. And he chose the *metaphor* of seasons — which unified the entire speech — to symbolize his lens of change; the lens through which he viewed America. Easy, but effective.

3.10: PRESENT ANTITHETICALS
What is it?

Answering not only what you stand *for*, but what you stand *against*. "Today, we face essentially the same choice we faced in 2000, though it may be even more obvious now, because John McCain – a man who has earned our respect on many levels – is now openly endorsing the policies of the Bush-Cheney White House and promising to actually continue them. The same policies all over again? Hey, I believe in recycling, but that's ridiculous. *With John McCain's support, President Bush and Vice President Cheney have led our nation into one calamity after another because of their indifference to fact; their readiness to sacrifice the long term to the short term, subordinate the general good to the benefit of the few and short-circuit the rule of law.*" – Al Gore

Why does it work?

It appeals to innate psychological drives: The drive to join a tribe, or a psychological coalition; a drive which demands both an in-group and an out-group; both a "who we are" and "who we are not." Every story

—

demands a villain. Every hero needs an antihero. A clearly defined antithetical satisfies all these psychological needs, making your message more captivating and compelling.

How do you do it?

What – and who – do you stand against? Why? What have they done that we would consider morally egregious?

STEP FOUR
IMPROVE YOUR VOCAL TONALITIES

___

4.1: USE BREAKING-RAPPORT TONALITY
What is it?

Ending a sentence on a lower pitch than the pitch with which you started it.

Why does it work?

It signals confidence. It signals you don't need a validating response. It signals a sort of authoritative "end of story" vibe. It signals certainty. It signals a sense of conclusion: When someone concludes their speaking without using this, there's an awkward silence as people are unsure whether or not they finished. It sounds like they "snipped" their speech prematurely.

How do you do it?

Use it when you are making substantive statements essential to your message.

4.2: USE OPEN-RAPPORT TONALITY
What is it?

Ending a sentence on a higher pitch than the pitch with which you started it, much like a question.

___

Why does it work?

It grabs attention. It captivates. It draws people into your communication. When you hear someone ask a question, you largely know it's a question because of the tonality: Because pitch ends higher than where it started. And when you hear someone asking you a question, you listen. Applying this tonality elsewhere achieves the same result. It signals the start of back-and-forth rapport, which holds our attention.

How do you do it?

Be warned: Questions signal uncertainty. And this tonality signals questions. So it subconsciously signals uncertainty. For the bulk of your communication, and when you're making essential substantive statements, use breaking rapport. But when you're making non-substantive statements – perhaps introductions, or basic logistic information like "turn your attention to this model" – use this tonality to build rapport and draw people in.

4.3: USE THE PROJECTION SPECTRUM
What is it?

Varying your volume of projection to achieve specific impacts on listeners.

Why does it work?

It layers meaning delivered through volume over meaning delivered through words. This is more compelling and captivating, transmitting ideas through both the realm of words – a largely conscious input-stream – and the domain of abstract sound, a largely subconscious input-stream.

How do you do it?

You're dealing with a spectrum. In fact, three spectrums: The pitch, pace, and projection spectrums, which we'll get into shortly. On one end of the projection spectrum you have low volume, and on the other you have high volume. In the middle is moderate volume. You impart different subconscious meanings at each point on this spectrum. How do you use it? How do you use all these spectrums? Learn the positions on the spectrum and the different effects they create (which I'll teach you). Identify which effect you want to create (and which extremities to avoid). Produce communication defined by the position on the spectrum creating the effect you want. So, let's get into it. Avoid extremely loud volume. This puts people on edge, making them feel the same flood of stress hormones produced when they are under physical assault. Avoid extremely quiet communication. This undermines your image, presenting the appearance of weakness. It also appears to lack confidence. Now, moderately quiet communication implies secrecy and scarcity of access to the exclusive, underground, "behind-the-scenes" information you're about to convey, inviting people into a "psychological conspiracy" of "sworn-secrecy." This captivates. It controls attention. And people often need to lean forward and listen intently, focusing deeply on you, giving you a compelling presence in the room. Moderately loud communication exudes confidence. It exudes a sense of natural leadership. It exudes a sense of doubtlessness. It portrays intensity and passion. It also captivates attention, not by forcing people to lean in and hush to hear you, but by guaranteeing they hear you no matter what. "Even" volume – at the middle of the spectrum – sounds conversational, exuding friendliness, casualness, and calm: Both relaxing people and portraying yourself as relaxed.

4.4: USE THE PITCH SPECTRUM
What is it?
Varying your pitch to achieve specific impacts on listeners.

Why does it work?
Layered meaning. Subconscious meaning. Specific effects on the audience. Same as the projection spectrum, and same as the pace spectrum which follows.

How do you do it?
Extremely deep pitch inhibits your ability to annunciate words, making them blur together and reducing your clarity. It also stretches your vocal capabilities to the limit, leaving little capacity for applying the other spectrums. You know you're operating in this extremity

if it feels unnatural. Extremely high pitch also feels unnatural. Both of them feel forced. And seeming like you're trying to deliberately modulate your pitch undermines the impacts and undermines your image. So avoid the two extremities. Moderately low pitch sounds authoritative. Commanding. Confident. Competent. Capable. Collected. Trustworthy. And I do not endorse this, but I recognize it as scientifically proven: Social norms suggest that men with deeper voices are more manly. Silly. But gentlemen: Lowering your voice – not unnaturally, but within the constraints of your normal pitch range – produces positive impacts. A potential side effect of deep pitch? It can sound threatening. The impacts of even pitch depends on what the middle of your pitch range is. If your even pitch tends to be deeper, it produces the associated effects. And if it tends to be higher, it produces the effects associated with high pitch. What are they? Higher pitches make you seem inviting, caring, personable, and nurturing. A higher pitch sounds less authoritative, but more kind. More forgiving. Accepting. Gentle. It's also easier to annunciate at higher pitches. And higher pitches cut through background noises easier. But remember: You don't choose one and stick with it. You move between them at different times and to create different impacts as desired, to augment the meaning of your word language with your vocal language.

4.5: USE THE PACE SPECTRUM
What is it?
Varying your pace to achieve specific impacts on listeners.

Why does it work?
Layered meaning. Subconscious meaning. Specific effects on the audience.

How do you do it?
Extremely fast pace loses people. It confuses them. It sounds unhinged and uncollected. It presents information faster than they can possibly take it in, leading them to give up on trying in the first place. Extremely slow pace bores people. All appropriate paces present information no faster and no slower than people

—

can take it in, while still creating different effects. And what are they? Moderately fast pace sounds energetic. It controls attention because if they don't tune in, they might miss something. But it doesn't lead to them actually missing something. It sounds intelligent. Sharp. It sounds like you're speaking this quickly because you think this quickly, or faster. It portrays command of the subject matter. Be careful when you present complex information quickly: Acceptably fast pace matched with complex information can quickly suffer the same ails as unacceptably fast pace. "Even" pace sounds reasonable. Moderate. Relaxed. Collected. Controlled. Slow pace is suited for evoking emotions; producing suspense; setting up for impact; emphasizing an idea. It also allows you to present complex information without losing people. But don't present simple information slowly: You'll lose them like that too. Some side effects to note: Talking fast can seem forceful. It can present you as a slick "hustler," someone smart enough to take advantage of people – and doing it. So present substantive information quickly; present logical information and evidence quickly. But when it comes to discussing

—

---

something emotional, something excessively human, do it slowly. When it comes for asking for action, do it slowly. And speaking too slowly can make you seem unintelligent. As if you're struggling to draw the information out. So when you're preventing your core substantive information, present it quickly.

4.6: USE TEXTURE
What is it?
Varying the texture of your voice to achieve specific impacts on listeners.

Why does it work?
I'll be honest: I don't know *why* certain sounds create certain impacts in people. But I know they do.

How do you do it?
There are too many textures, so I'll give you the all-encompassing principle that suggests the specific techniques on the spot: Think about corresponding sounds in the world and the associations tied to them. For example, a smooth and flowing texture evokes the

---

---

sound of a gentle stream. It relaxes. It calms. A deep, crackling texture sounds like a popping fireplace. It sounds crisp. It sounds satisfying. A raspy texture sounds like a growl. It gives you an edge. It portrays dangerous competence; deadly efficacy; threatening capability. The different vocal textures are boundless.

4.7: USE VOCAL CONTRASTS
What is it?

Contrasting elements of vocal variation with each other, and also matching contrasts of meaning with contrasts of modulation.

Why does it work?

We talked about why contrasts work. We talked about why vocal modulation works. Now let's put it together. Vocal contrasts match the inherent power of contrasts with corresponding verbal contrasts, portraying contrast with words and with voice; consciously (through words) and subconsciously (through voice).

———

How do you do it?

Here's an example: Let's say you want to present an obvious statement, followed by a little-known secret. You could create contrast with words like so: "The obvious truth is... But the little-known secret is..." How would you layer verbal contrasts over this? Deliver "the obvious truth" with a loud voice and quickly; deliver "the little-known secret" with a quiet voice – almost a whisper – and slowly. Get it?

4.8: USE "PPP" VARIATION
What is it?

Continually varying your pitch, pace, and projection throughout your communication.

Why does it work?

Patterns, continued excessively, lose attention. Variation creates intrigue and interest, drawing us in and captivating us by keeping us guessing. "PPP" variation avoids monotony; the biggest pitfall causing most people to lose the attention of their listeners.

———

How do you do it?

Apply the three spectrums all at once, moving up and down them, all three of them, at the same time. Constantly vary your position on each of the three spectrums to create unique and distinct effects.

4.9: USE INTENSE-CALM JUMPS
What is it?

Quickly jumping from intense vocal modulation to calm vocal modulation, or vice-versa.

Why does it work?

It grabs attention by suddenly breaking through an established pattern in an intense way. It's surprising. It's a JOLT if you go from calm to intense, but gentle and relaxing if you go from intense to calm.

How do you do it?

Use PPP variation towards the "calmer," less intense ends of the spectrums. Then suddenly, in a way aligned with the meaning of your words, rapidly jump to the intense ends of the spectrums.

4.10: USE EMPHASIS
What is it?

Using elements of your vocal modulation to place emphasis on a word, segment, sentence, or unit of meaning.

Why does it work?

It subconsciously imparts the following meaning: "this word, this idea, this concept, this unit of meaning; this deserves all your attention; this is what it's all about; this is the essential idea; this is the key; focus on it now."

How do you do it?

To emphasize a word, say the first syllable slightly louder than the other words in the sentence, make the pitch of the word either higher or lower than the other words in the sentence, say it slower than you normally would, stretch the vowel sound, and make a brief pause after you say it. And, as always, use your body to express the same sentiment as your voice; if you want to emphasize a word, do so with accompanying gestures as well.

STEP FIVE
IMPROVE YOUR BODY LANGUAGE

5.1: MASTER GESTURES
What is it?
Using the movements of your hands to impart meaning.

Why does it work?
It adds a third (or fourth) layer of communication, over words, vocal modulations, and visuals (if you have visuals).

How do you do it?
There are three principle modes of gesturing. First: Resting. No gestures. Your arms in their natural resting position. The "default." You don't want to "over-gesture." You want fewer gestures with more impact. The more you gesture, the less impact each gesture carries. So when you stay in the resting position, you do so to thread this balance. But you also don't want to remain in this default position for too long: Doing so prevents you from imparting meaning through gestures. The worst case is no gestures. A better case is random gestures. The best case is strategic gestures with high impact interspersed by periods in the resting position.

Second: Mirroring. Mirroring gestures seek to physically mirror the meaning of your words. Describing two opposing ideas? Hold your two fists up on either side. Shake each fist when you hit on the item it represents. Explaining where the two ideas come together? Bring your fists together. Listing a series of items? List them on your fingers. Describing something "pushing the frontier forward?" hold your hands out palms facing you, and push them forward, toward the audience. Presenting mock confusion? Throw your hands up. Want to emphasize that something is trapped? Wrap the fingers of your left hand around the index finger of your right hand, "trapping" it. You get the point. The examples are boundless. Third: Abstract. Abstract gestures do not mirror the meaning of your words. Instead, they create implicit impacts on the audience. For example, simply moving your hands gently in the rhythm of your vocal cadence draws people in. Or using the steeple, fingers of each hand touching the tip of the corresponding finger on the other hand, and holding this over your chest, subconsciously evokes power and competence. Also: If you have a video of yourself speaking, and you want to eliminate repetitive gestures (remember, excessive patterns kill), replay the video on maximum speed. Repetitive gestures will announce themselves.

5.2: MASTER OPEN POSTURE
What is it?

Carrying your body in a way that makes your torso open.

Why does it work?

Humans associate open posture with friendliness, approachability, influence, social status, comfort, confidence, and competence. Humans associate closed posture with inadequacy, insecurity, incompetency, fear, and anxiety. Open posture suggests an open person. Closed posture? A closed person. Why? Because our torsos contain our vital and most vulnerable organs. Tens of thousands of years ago, if we felt like we were in physical danger, we covered our torsos. When we felt safe, we left them open. Humans understand and perceive this intuitively, based on a learned correlation between "openness of posture" and the positive qualities produced by open posture.

How do you do it?

Don't block your torso. Face the audience. Keep your back straight. Broaden your shoulders. Cock back your shoulders. Gesture by your sides, not in front of your torso (at least most of the time). Keep your arms moderately wide; not stuck right up against your body, not stretched out like airplane wings, but somewhere in between, seemingly giving your torso "breathing room."

5.3: MASTER THE "ACA" TRIAD

What is it?

Activating, Controlling, and Aligning your three languages (words, voice, and body language): Making sure they are all active, under your deliberate control, and aligned in sentiment.

Why does it work?

First of all: If all your languages aren't activated, your communication becomes less impactful. You can't communicate with everything at your disposal unless you activate all your languages. Secondly: If all your languages aren't controlled, you can't ensure they produce the correct impact on the audience. You might be gesturing, but your gestures are producing the wrong impact. Finally: If all your languages aren't aligned, your body language might be saying one thing, your vocal language another, and your word language yet another. This makes you seem disingenuous. Speakers can easily manipulate their words. But signs of deceit sneak through, and can't easily be stifled, in a speaker's body language and vocal tonalities. So people are wired to pay attention to body language and vocal tonalities. And if they aren't aligned with your words, it signals deceit. If they aren't activated and controlled, you can't ensure they're aligned.

How do you do it?

The ACA triad applies to vocal tonalities too. But with respect to body language, you activate this language by using these techniques, you control this language by using these techniques to create a deliberate and specific

———

impact, and you align this language with your other languages by using these techniques to create a deliberate and specific impact cohesive with the impact of your words and vocal tonalities. This removes all dissonance between your three languages. Are your words spelling an upsetting scene? Let your voice show it. And your body language too, through strategic facial expressions and emotional gestures. Are your words suggesting confidence? Use confident body language and confident vocal tonalities.

5.4: MASTER MOVEMENT
What is it?
Moving around the room or area in which you're speaking.

Why does it work?
It acts as a pattern-interrupt. And since the closer you are the more engaging you are, by moving around the room you engage more people.

How do you do it?

You've been speaking from one side of the room? Take a gentle stroll to the other. Want to make three points? Move from one side of the room to the middle for your first transition (point one to two), and from the middle to the other side for your second transition (point two to three). This strategy is, of course, alignment as well. Don't be too brisk. And don't pace too often. But a gentle, smooth, controlled pace from one side of the room to the other, while talking, portrays confidence, competence, and command of the subject and situation. And remember this: When you're not moving, keep your feet planted to the floor.

5.5: MASTER EYE CONTACT
What is it?

Using eye contact to create a captivating presence.

Why does it work?

Eye contact captivates. Why? I'll be truthful: I don't know why. It's so ubiquitously true and outstandingly self-evident I never bothered to find out. But it earns trust. It forms a connection. It portrays credibility. It conveys good intentions. It carries dozens of benefits and no detriments.

How do you do it?

Now: It seems simple. It's another "just do it" situation. So I'll answer this question: When do you *not* make eye contact? When you want to signal introspection. When you want to signal that you're searching deep within yourself, producing an insight based on personal experience. And a key note for when you do make eye contact (70% or more of the time): When you shift your gaze, don't dart your eyes back and forth. That's called being "shifty-eyed." Gently, gracefully, and smoothly move your entire head, not just your eyes.

5.6: MASTER COMFORT GESTURES

What is it?

Avoiding subconscious gestures that undermine your physical presence.

Why does it work?

These comfort gestures signal anxiety. They happen when your mind feels you are unsafe (like when giving a presentation – one of the most feared scenarios), and it wants to subconsciously remind itself it has control over your physical body. How does it do that? By instigating these gestures.

How do you do it?

Comfort gestures are persistent and annoying. For example: Constantly tapping your feet when you speak (most comfort gestures happen with feet because when we take control of our body language, we tend to forget to extend physical awareness to our feet). Constantly checking your watch. Constantly fiddling with your clothes, jewelry, or hair. Constantly glancing in a certain direction. You get the idea. These are all mental attempts to remind yourself that you are in control of your physical environment, and that you retain physical autonomy. And this is only something your mind would every do when it's anxious. Anxious people tend to lack credibility. And listeners pick up on comfort gestures,

———

and realize, subconsciously and instantly, where they come from. One of the worst comfort gestures I witnessed? Someone took two steps forward. Two huge steps. Then two steps back. Then two steps forward. Big, leaping steps. Back and forth. Back and forth. Back and forth. The biggest irony? Everything else about his delivery conveyed confidence. But what's the key he missed out on? Alignment. Despite everything he did right, this one incongruency – this one misalignment – undermined our perception of him, revealing the anxiety bubbling just beneath the surface.

5.7: MASTER PHYSICAL PATTERN-INTERRUPTS
What is it?
Using pattern-interrupts in the domain of your body language.

Why does it work?
Patterns habituate. You know that by now.

How do you do it?
Identify your body language patterns. Break them.

———

5.8: MASTER YOUR WARDROBE

What is it?

Dressing strategically to signal both parity and authority.

Why does it work?

Parity – or similarity – and authority are essential characteristics of someone worth listening to. "He is a lot like me, and can understand me, but knows something I don't, thus has something to offer." Compare that to just parity: "He's just like me, and he can understand me, but he can't offer me much." And compare that to just authority: "He knows a lot I don't, but doesn't understand me or have anything in common with me, so he can't offer me much."

How do you do it?

Dress just one step above how your audience is dressed. Get it? This maintains both identifiability and authority as conveyed by what you're wearing.

5.9: MASTER RECEIVING NONVERBALS

What is it?

Understanding how to decode the communication your audience is sending your way.

Why does it work?

It allows you to react to their nonverbal signals.

How do you do it?

What are the actual, physical, observable signs an audience gives off? It can vary widely. They can sit forward in their seats, or lean back. They can look directly at you, or off to one of your sides. They can be fidgety, or they can be still. They can murmur to each other, or be totally silent. They can sigh or check their watches. They can either be responsive to your humor or not. They can show varying facial expressions, or be completely expressionless. Each of these signs communicate a different sentiment. If your audience is sitting on the edge of their seats, it can mean that they are highly attentive and engaged, but also that you may be speaking too quietly or too quickly and they need to

---

sit forward to hear more clearly. If you are sure it is not the latter, then this is a very good sign that your speech is a success. If they are looking at you, and returning your eye contact (which you should always have with your audience), it means that you have achieved an audience to speaker connection and that they are engaged with your speech. On the contrary, if they are looking to your sides or somewhere behind you, that means that they are distracted by something and you need to regain their attention. Similarly, if they are being fidgety, it can mean that they are bored by your speech or even that the temperature of the room is uncomfortable. This is one of the most telling signs of how an audience is receiving your speech, assuming that it doesn't have to do with the temperature. If your audience members are murmuring amongst themselves, it can mean that they are offended by the sentiment of your speech, or disagreeing with your message and voicing that disagreement to each other. One of the most obvious signals given by audience members, and in some cases one of the only ones that may be given consciously, is sighing and checking watches or phones for the time. It doesn't take

---

a behavioral psychologist to know that this means your speech is running a little long. If your audience responds to your humor, it means that you did a good job of establishing the speaker to audience connection early on. If they do not respond, it means the opposite. Lastly, your audience's facial expressions can say something about what's going through their heads. If you are painting a picture or describing an event that they find frustrating, they can grimace; a sign that they have good rapport established with you and are in agreement with your message. You should be concerned if you are indignantly relaying a frustrating situation and your audience is not grimacing. Similarly, you should be concerned if you are *not* relaying a frustrating situation and they *are* grimacing.

5.10: MASTER FACIAL EXPRESSIONS
What is it?
Activating one of the most compelling elements of body language: The meaning conveyed by your facial expression.

Why does it work?

Mirror neurons. We alluded to them previously. In short: We have neurons that simulate the feeling of doing what we see others doing, particularly what we see in their faces. So when someone sees *your* facial expression, their mirror neurons mirror the feeling of *them* making the same facial expression, recreating the emotion in them associated with the facial expressions.

How do you do it?

Let the emotions you genuinely feel about your subject express themselves in your facial expressions. Mirror neurons will do the rest.

STEP SIX
IMPROVE YOUR APPEAL

___

6.1: APPEAL TO VALUES

What is it?

Appealing to "favorite virtues" humans find innately, inherently, intrinsically, and inalienably valuable.

Why does it work?

We form groups based on common value hierarchies. And that which guaranteed our status as a group-member helped us survive thousands of years ago (and even today) which, in turn, led to natural selection for the proclivity to create and protect value hierarchies. Values are immensely compelling. They carry inherent persuasive appeal. They are beyond reason. They are assumed true and valuable. Freedom is an American value. Can anyone argue against freedom? Good luck. Some other examples of American values are generosity, innovation, hard work, education, hope, community, posterity, and lawfulness. We can't interact with people who have contrary value hierarchies and value systems. We don't know how. The United States and the Soviet Union nearly brought about nuclear mayhem due to

___

___

their contrary value systems. This conveys the immense power of values.

How do you do it?

Identify the applicable values which you can easily and naturally tie into your subject. Present your proposals and ideas as both stemming from the values and preserving the values; present them as ideas which the values create, and ideas which guarantee the values aren't breached. And never – and I mean never – run against values.

6.2: APPEAL TO EMOTION
What is it?

Appealing to emotional impulses and altering emotional states with emotionally stimulating communication.

Why does it work?

Humans are inherently emotional creatures. Aristotle recognized this when he identified emotion as the key to any persuasive endeavor. And here's the truth: Our emotions are foundational to successful living, acting as

___

———

a fundamental metronome through which we judge potential action-options. Our emotions are broadly categorized as "good" or "bad." And these signal, respectively, approach and avoidance. In the wilderness, 20,000 years ago, our ancestors needed to trust these emotional impulses to avoid gruesome deaths. The result? No matter how much we *think* it's right, if we don't *feel* it's right, we won't do it. And more often than not, if we don't feel like it's right, we'll never think it's right, no matter how logical and full-proof the substantive case is.

How do you do it?

There are countless strategies evoking emotion. The most powerful? Expressing *your* emotion. Why? Mirror neurons. People have a neurological proclivity to mirror the emotional states they observe in others. So to create an emotion in your audience, express that emotion yourself: In your voice, with your body language, and with your words.

6.3: APPEAL TO HEURISTICS

What is it?

Appealing to the rough "measuring sticks" we use to easily "answer" complex questions.

Why does it work?

Humans perform attribute substitution. This is a proven and systematic feature of human psychology, perception, judgement-making, and cognition. How does it work? We try to evaluate a hard question. We substitute an easy question, answer it, and transfer the answer of the easy question to the hard question, without even realizing it. In short: Instead of evaluating the *target* attribute, we evaluate a *heuristic* or *substitute* attribute and pretend like they are the same thing. Why? To lower cognitive load, and get a "good enough" judgement quickly. The evolutionary machinery behind this should be clear: Fast, snappy heuristic judgements gave us mental agility when mental sluggishness meant death. And so we have a genetic proclivity to produce the same cognitive processes for fast thinking today,

---

even when slower, more precise, and more logical thought would serve us better.

How do you do it?

Summarizing decades of groundbreaking cognitive-behavioral research by the two gifted researchers Daniel Kahneman and Amos Tversky, humans have a "system one" and a "system two." System one refers to fast, intuitive, and instinctual mental process; the mental processes relying on rough short-cuts like biases and heuristics to subconsciously get immediate results with little effort. System two? System two refers to our analytical mind, dealing with complicated situations system one can't manage, and doing so slowly, deliberately, and carefully. Math. Complex analysis of any kind. That's system two. System two expends calories, and when we are physically tired, it doesn't work as well, and we bounce back to system one when we shouldn't. What's our default? System one. What triggers a switch to system two? High stakes and unintuitive subject matter; new, uncomfortable situations demanding slow deliberative thought. Want to influence and persuade with sophisticated strategy that creates an irresistible psychological pull towards your ideas? Speak to both systems. I call this bimodal influence, including both system one messaging (appealing to snap judgements, intuitive, bias- and heuristic-driven subconscious cognitive functions) and system two messaging (appealing to deep, deliberate, and effortful cognitive functions). People always live in one of the two. Bimodal influence guarantees your communication hits home with everyone. And it's drastically, dramatically more effective. System one messaging targets heuristic attributes (which people substitute for the target attribute). System one messaging is three-step persuasion: You hit the heuristic attribute, people substitute the heuristic attribute for the target attribute, and thus people perceive the target attribute. For example: You make your proposal literature aesthetically pleasing, people substitute "good looking" for "good," and thus people find your proposal good (and yes, aesthetic appeal is a common heuristic attribute). The algorithm for achieving bimodal influence by speaking to system one? ASA: Attribute substitution activation. The step-by-step process? Step one: Identify the question you are trying to answer with your communication. For example, maybe you want to answer the question "is [insert your idea] a good idea?" And you want to answer it with a resounding "yes," not in your mind, but in your audience's minds. Step two: Identify the probable heuristic attributes people will substitute for your target attribute. Step three: Maximize perception of those heuristic attributes (system one messaging), instead of only hitting the target attribute directly (system two messaging). This demands that you understand common heuristic attributes. Some frequent examples? People frequently substitute success on these following metrics for "how good, true, valuable, and important the idea is:" How intuitive the idea is, how simple the idea is, how much evidence supposedly supports the idea (independent from how good the evidence is or whether it actually supports the claim), how the idea makes them feel, how the speaker looks conveying the idea, how the speaker sounds conveying the idea, if they like the source of the idea, if the idea supports their preexisting worldviews.

6.4: APPEAL TO REPUTATION
What is it?
Appealing to people's reputation – real or fabricated by you – that they act how you want them to act.

Why does it work?
Psychological identity is an immensely powerful force. Humans desire identity. We want to know who we are. And when we get a sense of self-identity, we do anything to validate it. Identity is the key to action for this reason: People who are (insert identity) act in (insert ways). Every identity carries associations to patterns of action. In addition, the positive emotion of feeling a strong identity triggers the approach impulse.

How do you do it?
"Since you have a reputation for (insert pattern of action), may you please (insert related request)?" Or "I heard from a few people that you're (insert pattern of action). Do you think you could (insert related request)?"

6.5: APPEAL TO THE "WIIFM?" QUESTION

What is it?

Appealing to people's self-interest by answering the question "What's in it for me?"

Why does it work?

Human beings are vessels for genetic material. And genetic material is extremely selfish. All it "wants" is to replicate itself. Traits carried by genetic material that failed to replicate itself died out. Traits carried by genetic material that replicated itself lived on, becoming ubiquitous in the human species. And what could be more conducive to survival than looking out for one's own well-being? Now: Humans aren't always "selfish." Why not? Because, often, the best thing for the self is cooperative and generous pro-social behavior. But it all comes down to what's best for self, even if it seems selfless on the surface.

How do you do it?

Answer the "WIIFM" question. It's that simple. Tell them what's in it for them.

6.6: APPEAL TO HUMAN DESIRES

What is it?

Appealing to innate human desires engineered into us by hundreds of thousands of years of genetic evolution layered over thousands of years of cultural evolution.

Why does it work?

Certain desires led to survival. Over tens of thousands of years (or more), we evolved to have those desires. It's the same process by which self-interest became the dominant force behind human action. (This describes the bulk of desires, though some of them can stem from different sources).

How do you do it?

Identify a relevant human desire (the limited-edition bonus list of 197 human desires will be helpful here). Present your proposal or idea as satisfying the desire, preventing the dissatisfaction of the desire, or both.

___

6.7: APPEAL TO CONSISTENCY
What is it?

Appealing to the human tendency to want to act and think in ways consistent with past actions and patterns of thought.

Why does it work?

People are proven to do drastically extreme things if they perceive it as consistent with their previous actions. Why? I can think of a few evolutionary explanations: Consistency is predictable, making interpersonal relations less deadly; consistency saves mental energy (instead of redoing all the judgement, quickly ceding to the past self); consistency is based on learned correlations between "acting this way" and "surviving and thriving / not getting hurt."

How do you do it?

"Since you already did (insert first action), (insert second action), and (insert third action) the next step is (insert consistent request)."

___

6.8: APPEAL TO COGNITIVE BIASES
What is it?
Appealing to predictable, systematic, consistent, repetitive patterns of human judgement known as cognitive biases.

Why does it work?
Remember the core mantra. These biases are ingrained in human psychology. They dominate our thinking. They are damn-near unavoidable. The result? Tailoring your communication to work with the flow of these biases, turning them on in your favor instead of against you, is an immensely powerful persuasive strategy, producing instant influence.

How do you do it?
See your limited-edition bonus titled "25 cognitive biases" for an expanded discussion of how to do so.

6.9: APPEAL TO SOCIAL PROOF
What is it?
Appealing to the human tendency to follow the crowd.

―――

Why does it work?

Pro-social behavior is pro-survival behavior. Pro-survival behavior becomes human behavior (so too with any life form). Wanting to do as the crowd does made us more likely to do as the crowd, thus more likely to be accepted in the crowd, thus more likely to survive. And it's also a heuristic (as many of these different "appeals" are): We substitute the heuristic attribute "what others are doing" for the target attribute "what I should do" to conserve mental resources and keep cognitive load down (another evolutionary advantage).

How do you do it?

"10,000 people signed up just in the last week. X% of people think Y. 90% of people started doing X."

6.10: APPEAL WITH POWER WORDS
What is it?

Appealing to various components of human psychology and invoking myriad human desires with inherently powerful words.

___

Why does it work?

Certain words carry inherent appeal. Why? Because they inherently imply a sentiment deeply attractive to humans. The examples are countless. But some power words are more powerful than others.

How do you do it?

There are thousands of power words (and power phrases). Some of my favorite? Certainty power words: *Proven. Scientifically proven. Undeniably, unequivocally, and unambiguously proven. Guaranteed.* Ease power words: *Easy. Fast. Quick. Instant. Step-by-step. Simple.* Novelty power words: *New. Revolutionary. Uncovered. Groundbreaking.* Secrecy power words: *Little-known. Hidden. Underground. Secret.* Exclusivity power words: *Expert. Advanced. Exclusive. Rare. Proprietary. Scarce.*

___

STEP SEVEN
IMPROVE YOUR VISUALS

7.1: AVOID BLOCKS OF TEXT

What is it?

Avoiding text-overloaded slides.

Why does it work?

People listen if they perceive the net result of listening (that is, benefit minus cost) to be positive, and more positive than any alternatives. The net benefit drops if you use big blocks of text because the big blocks of text raise cost: They force people to expend more mental energy to get the same message. Chances are, many people simply won't. They also confuse people: Should they listen to you? Or read? Or try (and ultimately fail) to do both?

How do you do it?

Ask yourself this question: "If I could summarize this entire paragraph of text in three sentences, what would those three sentences be?"

7.2: AVOID COMPLEX SENTENCES
What is it?
Avoiding complex sentences on slides.

Why does it work?
It works for the same reasons as avoiding text-overloaded slides. In short: Complex sentences raise cost of paying attention by demanding more attention to interpret the same meaning. If cost exceeds benefit, people won't pay attention. And if an alternative exists with a better balance of benefits and costs – a higher net payoff – they'll pay attention to that, getting distracted from you.

How do you do it?
After cutting big paragraphs and replacing them with three sentences (with plenty of empty white space between them), ask yourself this of each sentence: "How could I cut the length of this sentence in half but impart the same essential meaning?"

—

7.3: AVOID OFF-PUTTING AESTHETICS

What is it?

Avoiding "clever" and complicated visuals.

Why does it work?

Chances are you don't have a degree in graphic design. Chances are trying to create the visual compositions of the slides yourself will lead to off-putting aesthetics. Getting the visuals right carries two tremendous benefits: First of all, "aesthetic appeal" is a heuristic variable for all sorts of target variables, like "truthfulness, relevance, salience, importance, credibility…" Second of all, well-composed aesthetics lower perceived cost; they lower the predicted cognitive load of taking in the information. They make it seem easier to take in the information on the slides, so more people will read them. And they do this without changing any of the information; just how it's presented.

How do you do it?

The two big slide-creating softwares, PowerPoint and Google Slides, offer a massive number of premade

—

templates. Use those. It'll save time. Don't trick yourself into thinking you can make anything better. And if you're not sure which one to pick, go with the simplest one; the one that's easiest on the eyes (because it's also easiest on the mind, and the mind craves ease).

7.4: AVOID READING THE SLIDES
What is it?
Avoiding reading directly from the slides.

Why does it work?
It's terrible. It's just… terrible. And so many people do it. There's no faster way to bore an audience to death. The expression "death by PowerPoint" is coined because of how many people make this critical error. Remember: Your audience can read. And believe me: They know you can read. No need to prove yourself. Do they read the slides in their heads? Or listen to you? Or both? Nobody knows. Reading slides kills your vocal tonalities. It kills your presence. It saps your charisma. It's the big thing to avoid. It expresses anxiety, lack of confidence, and a weak grasp of the subject matter.

How do you do it?

Remember: Speakers read the slides because they're anxious. And they're anxious because they don't know what they're talking about. So research the subject. Know what you're talking about. Know it so well it becomes a part of you, called upon fluently and easily. You won't need to defer to the slides.

7.5: AVOID USING IT AS A CRUTCH
What is it?

Avoiding using the slides a "crutch," beyond reading directly from them.

Why does it work?

Reading directly from the slides is the extreme form of using them as a crutch. A less extreme form? Not knowing what to say next until you switch to the next slide so the header can remind you of the next "step." Here's the truth: People can tell when you're using the slides as a crutch. And would you trust someone who's using a crutch to help you walk through a subject? Probably not.

How do you do it?

Research. But what if you're so pressed for time you end up being forced into a situation where you have to use the slides as a crutch? Be subtle with it. Make the best of a bad situation. Glance at the header quickly. Do everything you can to conceal that you need to look at the header to know what to say.

7.6: USE META-SIGNPOSTS
What is it?

Using meta-signposting to create slide content. What's meta-signposting? It tells your audience information about what you're saying. For example, let's say you're going to paint a problem, discuss a few solutions to the problem, present their failings, present your superior solution, and then present the proof of concept. Your slides could read as follows: (1) "The problem..." (2) "The industry solutions..." (3) "The problems with the solutions..." (4) "A better way..." (5) "The proof..."

Why does it work?

People tune-out. Even the best speakers occasionally lose attention. So: The metric for success is not whether or not you lose attention. Instead, we measure success like so: How few people drift away? When they drift away, is it on a train of thought related to your subject? (If they stopped listening because they're imagining themselves using your idea and loving it, that's not bad at all). For how long did they drift before you brought them back? And when they stop drifting of their own accord, is it easy for them to see where you are and join you again? Meta-signposting tells people information about what you're saying, making it easy for them to "reenter" your world seamlessly. And meta-signposting is just about the only kind of content you can use as a crutch. Why? Because it's a crutch to the structure and sequence of the information; not the information itself. It doesn't indicate any shortcomings in your command of the subject. And it can help you maintain a structure that gets results, ensuring you aren't missing steps or weakening the inherent power of the structure by blurring steps together.

―――

How do you do it?

Identify the steps in your structure. Make a slide for each step. Write the step on that slide. You're done. Easy, right? And remember: The structures I presented were top-level structures. You can break them down to a greater level of specificity if you need to. The example I gave you of meta-signposting was a Problem, Agitate, Solution structure with a few extra steps injected in between. Remember this too: If you're using the Victim, Perpetrator, Benevolence structure, should you write "Victim, Perpetrator, Benevolence" on your slides? Of course not. The structures I gave you in step one are presented in a way suited for communicators, not communication receivers. Most receivers would be put off, even offended, if you signposted "Victim, Perpetrator, Benevolence" that way, ruining the power of the structure. Instead, for this structure, you should make it "(1) It's unjust and unfair... (2) Who breached justice? (3) How can we make it right again?" Use your judgement when signposting.

―――

7.7: USE SHORT, SNAPPY SENTENCES

What is it?

Using short sentences.

Why does it work?

It lowers cognitive load.

How do you do it?

Exactly how I presented 7.7.

7.8: USE IMAGES

What is it?

Replacing word-dominated slides with image-dominated slides.

Why does it work?

You can convey words. You can't convey images. At least not as well as an image projected on a screen. Don't use your slides to do what you can do better; use them to do what they can do better. And humans are predominantly visual creatures. Which of your five senses gives you the most information about your

---

environment? Exactly. And, as you know, you must convey information how the human mind is wired to receive it.

How do you do it?

Replace all words with images. Or most of the words if you're not ready for that yet. And make sure the images are high-resolution. Make them fill the screen too: No edges of the slide should peak out from behind the image. You can layer meta-signposting with image-driven slides. How? The only words on the slides are words about the words you're speaking, and the slides in between are images visualizing what you're saying.

7.9: USE "HOOK" SLIDES

What is it?

Slides designed solely to hook audience attention.

Why does it work?

It guarantees "attention-command" throughout your communication.

———

How do you do it?

Create slides with the ten hooks in the next step.

7.10: USE GAP SLIDES

What is it?

Empty slides acting as gaps between meaningful slides.

Why does it work?

It limits the number of inputs competing for attention. Let's say people perceive two equivalently captivating inputs: They each get 50% of attention. Three? 33% each. One? 100%. It's a different dynamic between non-equivalent inputs, but it follows the same essential rule of attention-dilution: The more inputs people perceive, the less attention each of those inputs gets. And you want full attention. So: Most people who aren't ready to move to the next slide will project a slide they don't need anymore, thus sustaining an input that dilutes attention. Using a "gap slide" shuts down this competing input and prevents attention dilution, giving you 100% of attention (theoretically). And let's say you're projecting images: If people realize you put gap slides between images, they'll

———

direct intense attention to the image because they know it'll shortly be replaced by a blank side.

How do you do it?

It's simple: Put a gap slide where you think you'll need one. It can be totally blank, or it can be a slide from the template, with the same visual composition, without any content on it. This latter option maintains visual continuity.

STEP EIGHT
IMPROVE YOUR HOOK

8.1: ASK A QUESTION
What is it?

Hooking audience attention by asking a rhetorical question that you're going to subsequently answer.

Why does it work?

It plays upon innate human curiosity.

How do you do it?

"What does X reveal about Y? Why does X happen? How do some X get Y, while others get Z?" The possibilities are boundless.

8.2: BREAK A BELIEF
What is it?

Hooking audience attention by breaking a common belief they likely hold about your subject.

Why does it work?

It creates an "open-loop" by poking a hole in the audience's intellectual status-quo; a hole they'll shortly want to fill. How? By listening to you. It also causes

---

cognitive dissonance, which is emotionally arousing; and emotional arousal controls attention.

How do you do it?

"Here's the brutal truth about X: Despite what everyone says, Y isn't true. And I can prove it to you."

8.3: PRESENT A TIME-STAMPED PROMISE
What is it?

Hooking audience attention by presenting an explicit or implicit promise of protection from pain or attainment of pleasure, within a snappy time-frame.

Why does it work?

People want to improve their lives. And if listening to you is promised to offer them a way to do so, they will. They also want to improve their lives with minimal effort. And the short time-frame implies minimal effort.

How do you do it?

"Give me five minutes and I'll show you how to get X / avoid X."

8.4: INVITE A SIMULATION
What is it?

Hooking audience attention by inviting them to imagine a simulation related to your subject.

Why does it work?

Mental simulations are immensely captivating. Conveyed correctly, we can't fully resist getting fully wrapped up in the simulation.

How do you do it?

Say the magic word "imagine," and then paint the simulation for them.

8.5: PRESENT PLEASURE MINUS PLAIN
What is it?

Hooking audience attention by simultaneously raising pleasure and lowering pain with a simple speaking pattern.

Why does it work?

This particular speaking pattern plays on the "towards pleasure away from pain" algorithm of human action in a uniquely compelling way.

How do you do it?

"Want to get X without dealing with Y?"

8.6: TEASE NOVELTY

What is it?

Hooking audience attention by teasing the reveal of new information.

Why does it work?

In the critically acclaimed show *Mad Men*, the main character Don Draper says "The most important word in advertising is *new*." He was right. Novelty commands our attention, captivating us and building anticipation for something new.

How do you do it?

"Do you know the new method to X? What's the new insight X reveals about Y? What's the revolutionary way to get X?"

8.7: START WITH A PROBLEM
What is it?

Hooking audience attention by starting with the problem you solve.

Why does it work?

It builds emotional resonance right from the beginning by referencing a problem; a problem associated with emotional pain. Remember how neural associations work? Two neurons or neural clumps associated with each other activate simultaneously. Touch on one and the other activates too. How does the association first form? It forms when the two neurons or neural clumps fire up at the same time. Eventually, they link: Hit one, they both light up. And because the problem is linked to negative emotion, simply mentioning it will create negative emotion (of course, you can explicitly call it out

---

too: "do you feel...?") People move away from pain. So they'll listen if they perceive you as offering an escape from the pain created by the thought of the problem.

How do you do it?

"Do you struggle with X? Most people who are X struggle with Y. Chances are you're constantly dealing with X and hating it."

8.8: PRESENT SECRECY

What is it?

Hooking audience attention by implying the reveal of a big secret; of insider information; of a little-known insight.

Why does it work?

We have an innate drive to acquire the scarce. The rare. The in-demand. The exclusive. This applies to the information we seek too.

How do you do it?

"What are the experts of X not telling us? Do you know the hidden, little-known, underground secrets of X? What's the little-known method to get X?"

8.9: AGREE AND AVAIL
What is it?

Hooking audience attention by agreeing with their biggest pain-point and promising to avail them of it.

Why does it work?

It builds empathy and portrays authority: The two qualities of someone worth listening to.

How do you do it?

"Do you struggle with X? I did too. Does X make you feel Y? It felt like this for me too. Let me show you how I solved X…"

———

8.10: PRESENT A FORK IN THE ROAD

What is it?

Hooking audience attention by presenting your subject as a fork in the road; the difference between success and failure.

Why does it work?

High stakes instigate attention. And presenting your subject as the difference between success and failures indicates high stakes.

How do you do it?

"What's the single thing separating success and failure in X? What separates successful and outstanding X from their average counterparts? Why do some X struggle to get Y, while others get it with less work?" And a brief note: You can layer all of these. And I don't mean just two or three at once. But all ten. You don't have to. But you can. And you can use these whenever you want to grab attention, not only at the start.

———

STEP NINE
IMPROVE YOUR ELOQUENCE

9.1: USE ALLITERATION

What is it?

Words in close proximity starting with the same sound create alliteration: "And so I say to all of us here, let us resolve to reform our *p*olitics, so that *p*ower and *p*rivilege no longer shout down the voice of the *p*eople. Let us *p*ut aside *p*ersonal advantage so that we can feel the *p*ain and see the *p*romise of America." – Bill Clinton

Why does it work?

Remember: A heuristic variable is something people substitute in for a target variable, assuming they stand for each other. A common heuristic? Processing fluency substituting for truth: "A statement I processed easily is more likely to be true." This is a subconscious judgement. And people automatically, systematically, predictably and subconsciously substitute the easy question, "how fluently do I process this information?" for the hard question, "how true, important, and valuable is this information?" transferring the answer from the first to the second. Why? To conserve mental energy, a key function of countess psychological

---

processes hammered into us by 200,000 years of evolution. And alliteration increases processing fluency. See how it all comes together? It's called the rhyme as reason effect. It's well-researched. Countless studies prove that alliteration and other strategies that raise processing fluency raise perception of truth.

How do you do it?

Of course, if you're speaking from a prepared manuscript, these eloquence techniques are easy. So I'll talk about how to use them extemporaneously. Consider your word-choice carefully. Prior to speaking, consider your message. Practice delivering it. Write down what you said. And introduce some alliterative elements. Now, practice saying those. They will cement themselves in your mind. A more flexible alternative is quickly considering your next word in the moment, and managing to select an appropriate and alliterative one without altering the flow of your speech.

9.2: USE ANTITHESIS

What is it?

Saying what something is not before saying what it is: "We choose to go to the moon in this decade and do the other things, *not* because they are easy, *but* because they are hard…" – John F. Kennedy

Why does it work?

It's memorable. Another heuristic is availability: People assume a message they recalled quickly is more truthful and important. And it's also mentally interactive, controlling attention in the moment. Why? Because by saying what something is not, you allow people to assume what it is (which many minds will automatically do), and when you break or meet this expectation, they feel drawn into your message.

How do you do it?

It's simple. It's self-evident. And it's extremely easy, in my view. How do you do it? Just say what something is not. Then say what it is. Fill in this simple formula, just like JFK: "…not X, but Y…"

9.3: USE ANAPHORA

What is it?

Starting subsequent sentences, segments, or units of meaning with the same words: "Even though large tracts of Europe and many old and famous States have fallen or may fall into the grip of the Gestapo and all the odious apparatus of Nazi rule, *we shall* not flag or fail. *We shall* go on to the end, *we shall fight* in France, *we shall fight* on the seas and oceans, *we shall fight* with growing confidence and growing strength in the air, *we shall* defend our Island, whatever the cost may be, *we shall fight* on the beaches, *we shall fight* on the landing grounds, *we shall fight* in the fields and in the streets, *we shall fight* in the hills; *we shall* never surrender..."

Why does it work?

It builds rhythm. Rhythm captivates. And it engineers repetition into your language. Repetition raises ease of processing, fluency, availability, and that whole clump of related heuristics people use to identify whether they will believe or disbelieve a message.

How do you do it?

It's simple. Identify a phrase essential to your message. Maybe you want people to believe they will succeed. The essential phrase? "We will succeed." Now expand it into an anaphora paradigm: "We will succeed because... We will succeed because... We will succeed because..." Continue as needed. This one is also easy to deliver extemporaneously. And of course, if you think you can automatically engineer these strategies into your speech simply by being aware of them, then do so.

9.4: USE MICRO-REPETITION
What is it?

Repetition of a word: "To renew America, we must meet challenges abroad as well at home. There is no longer division between what is foreign and what is domestic; the *world* economy, the *world* environment, the *world* AIDS crisis, the *world* arms race; they affect us all." – Bill Clinton

___

Why does it work?

The same reason as anaphora: Repetition builds rhythm and raises availability of the idea, making it seem more truthful, and making it "overweighed." Repetition makes the idea more memorable. And repetition activates the rhyme as reason effect. I prefer calling it the eloquence as truth effect. Repetition also emphasizes an idea, driving it home with greater impact. And, fascinatingly, repetition also activates the illusory truth effect: Studies prove an idea repeated multiple times is perceived as more truthful and accurate.

How do you do it?

Say the same word multiple times in different contexts. This one is easy. It's sort of a "just do it" kind of thing. If that doesn't satisfy you, do what Clinton did (though this is just one of myriad forms of micro-repetition): Select an adjective to repeat ("world" in Clinton's) and precede a sequence of nouns with that adjective. This might make it easier to naturally include micro-repetition in a fluent and relevant way.

___

9.5: USE SENTENTIA

What is it?

Summarizing preceding material in a particularly compelling sentence: "If we could first know where we are, and whither we are tending, we could then better judge what to do, and how to do it. We are now far into the fifth year, since a policy was initiated, with the avowed object, and confident promise, of putting an end to slavery agitation. Under the operation of that policy, that agitation has not only, not ceased, but has constantly augmented. In my opinion, it will not cease, until a crisis shall have been reached, and passed. *A house divided against itself cannot stand.*" – Abraham Lincoln

Why does it work?

Rhyme as reason. Fluency. Ease of processing as truth. You know the deal. It also works as a memory anchor. People draw from their memory in a cascade related to the subject that first prompted them. They draw on a first item in memory, and then memories linked to that memory, and then memories linked to *that* memory in a sort of ever-growing shotgun search. A message might be hard to remember. A *sententia* summarizing it is significantly easier. Thus, it's a memory anchor acting as a "stepping stone" to complete recall: People start the cascade, hit on the *sententia* summary, start cascading off of it, and hit on the entirety of the message linked to it. Simple, but fascinating.

How do you do it?

It's another "just do it" sort of thing. Even extemporaneously, it's quite easy to include. Ask yourself: How can I summarize my preceding message in a short, punchy, eloquent and hard-hitting sentence?

9.6: USE INTERROGATIVE CASCADES
What is it?

A sequence of rhetorical questions form an interrogative cascade: "Can anyone look at the record of this Administration and say, 'Well done?' Can anyone compare the state of our economy when the Carter Administration took office with where we are today and say, 'Keep up the good work?' Can anyone look at our

---

reduced standing in the world today and say, 'Let's have four more years of this?'" – Ronald Reagan

Why does it work?

The human mind is innately wired to cling to questions. Questions focus the scope of human cognition, and we take them in, play with them, consider them, and look at them from every angle, often without meaning to, often subconsciously. Further, questions functions much like an epiphany story: We hear the question, ponder it, and come to the answer the speaker wants us to come to. Series of questions emphasize the sentiment with more intensity, captivate attention, and build rhythm while making the self-evidence of the answer abundantly clear.

How do you do it?

If you can ask a rhetorical question, you can set up an interrogative cascade. Just ask a series of rhetorical questions, each hinting at a similar answer.

9.7: USE DECLARATORY CASCADES
What is it?

A series of short, commanding sentences or segments of sentences with relatively parallel grammatical structures and fairly direct syntax. Churchill's "we shall never surrender" passage shown previously was also a declaratory cascade.

Why does it work?

It creates an intense rhythm that draws the audience in. It also delivers a sequence of syntactically simple sentences, which lowers cognitive load. Why is this good? Because if cognitive load gets too high, people tune out. And processing fluency (linked to perception of truth by heuristic substitution) goes down, too.

How do you do it?

Deliver a sequence of sentences, all with simple and relatively parallel structures. For example: "X [verb]s Y," times five. "X breaches justice. X hurts Americans. X undermines our values. X raises inequality. And X harms our reputation."

___

9.8: USE A KEYSTONE SENTENCE
What is it?

A sentence summarizing the key idea repeated in its exact form with intervening material: "When a mother cannot spend time with her newborn child during the first weeks and months of that baby's life, and is forced back to work because her employer doesn't offer paid family leave and she can't afford not to work, that is not a family value. *That is an attack on everything that a family is supposed to stand for.* When a husband cannot get time off from work to care for his cancer-stricken wife or gravely ill child, that is not a family value. *That is an attack on everything that a family is supposed to stand for.* When a mother is force to send her sick child to school because her employer doesn't provide sick time and she cannot afford to stay home, that is not a family value. *That is an attack on everything that a family is supposed to stand for.* When a husband, wife, and kids, during the course of an entire year, are unable to spend any time together on vacation – that is not a family value. *That is an attack on everything that a family is supposed to stand for.*" – Bernie Sanders

___

___

Why does it work?

Repetition. Rhythm. Fluency. Availability. Rhyme as reason. Illusory truth. Ease of processing. You know the deal by now.

How do you do it?

Identify a sentence summarizing your message perfectly. Deliver an example, then state the sentence. Another example. Repeat the sentence. Another example. Repeat the sentence. Continue as needed.

9.9: USE OPPOSING PHRASES
What is it?

Using words that contrast each other: "Today, a generation raised in the *shadows* of the *Cold War* assumes *new responsibilities* in a *world warmed* by the *sunshine* of *freedom* but *threatened still* by *ancient hatreds* and *new plagues*."
– Bill Clinton

Why does it work?

Human perception functions through contrasts. Want to influence? Want to speak with eloquence? Want to hold

---

complete and captivated attention? Deliver information the way human minds are wired to receive it: By perceiving contrasts, which announce themselves to human perception and hook our attention.

How do you do it?

Observe how Clinton does it. Clinton contrasts shadows with sunshine, the Cold War with a world warmed, warmed with threatened, new responsibilities with ancient hatreds and new plagues, and ancient hatreds with new plagues.

9.10: USE ATTACHED ADJECTIVES
What is it?

Adjectives directly next to the noun they modify: "On this day, we gather because we have chosen hope over fear, unity of purpose over conflict and discord. On this day, we come to proclaim an end to the *petty* grievances and *false* promises, the recriminations and *worn-out* dogmas that for far too long have strangled our politics. We remain a young nation. But in the words of Scripture, the time has come to set aside childish

———

things. The time has come to reaffirm our *enduring* spirit; to choose our *better* history; to carry forward that *precious* gift, that *noble* idea passed on from generation to generation: the *God-given* promise that all are equal, all are free, and all deserve a chance to pursue their full measure of happiness." – Barack Obama

Why does it work?

What is more compelling? Grievances? Or petty grievances? Dogmas? Or worn-out dogmas? Spirit? Or enduring spirit? History? Or better history? Gift? Or precious gift? Idea? Or noble idea? Promise? Or God-given promise?

How do you do it?

Identify all your nouns and verbs. Precede them with an evocative and hard-hitting adjective, illuminating an essential element of the subject.

———

STEP TEN
IMPROVE YOUR MINDSET

10.1: COMMAND THE SUBJECT
What is it?

Command is competence. The most obvious and most powerful mindset shift is to shift from an incompetent mind to a competent one. What do I mean by that? I mean research your subject until you become more knowledgeable about it than 99% of others, except for experts who devote their careers to it.

Why does it work?

Command creates confidence. And confidence enables you to effortlessly and naturally use the techniques disclosed in this book, accomplishing the ten steps with ease. And command shows. People see who knows what they're talking about. Always.

How do you do it?

Identify your subject. Open up a document. Put it on the right side of your screen. Open up a search engine on the left. In the document, brainstorm every possible "sub-topic" related to your big topic. Now: Create a separate search engine tab for each of these subtopics, including searches like "[sub topic] statistics." Open the top five to ten search results for each of the subtopics. If you have ten subtopics, you should have around ten tabs, which turn into 50-100 when you open the top five-ten search results in each tab. Read them all, taking notes in the appropriate section of your document. Go to Google Scholar for original research, repeating the process there if need be. The abstracts of studies are quick summaries of results: Use their brevity to your advantage. Now review your document compiled from this research two or three, or maybe twelve or thirteen times. Not only is this going to guarantee you command of the subject, but it's also the type of in-depth research nearly nobody does, and it empowers your professional and personal development like nothing else.

10.2: BE THE NICEST PERSON IN THE ROOM
What is it?
People who seek influence through force fail and lose it. People who elevate others get elevated.

Why does it work?

Nobody respects someone who tries to "strong-arm" them, trying to exert control by the sheer force of their personality. Everyone respects the person who respects them. Everyone respects the nicest person in the room. And those who have respect have influence. And those with influence can communicate well.

How do you do it?

It's a mental shift. It happens in your mind. It's a constant self-reminder. It's a reminder to bring in the quiet voices, ensuring they get their say. It's a reminder to approach disagreements with an overabundance of friendliness. It's a reminder to recognize – and verbally validate – everyone's perspectives. It's a reminder not to speak longer than you need to solely for the sake of speaking, instead hearing what others need to say. It's a reminder to understand – not bend to, but understand – the emotions, desires, goals, fears, objectives, aversions, affinities, and worldviews of others, seeing things through their eyes. It's a commitment to exuding cooperative – not coercive – energy.

10.3: STOP TRYING

What is it?

Trying too hard will undermine you, bringing you further from the goals you overexerted yourself to reach. Try. Don't try too hard. Trust yourself and loosen the reigns.

Why does it work?

Communication is part art part science. It is extremely complex, with all the complexity crunched into a milli-second by milli-second situation. Trying too hard is a conscious exercise. But here's the brutal truth: Our conscious minds can't cope with the milli-second by milli-second complexity. But we're lucky. Our subconscious minds can. The problem? Trying too hard is proven to suppress our subconscious functioning.

How do you do it?

Imprint your goal and purpose in your head, focusing on it as you naturally would. But then let it go. Your subconscious mind will take over. You'll go further and feel like you aren't trying. Why? Because your conscious

---

———

mind – which is activated by trying too hard – will be out of the way, letting your subconscious mind – which is suppressed by trying too hard – take over. As it should.

10.4: APPRECIATE THE OPPORTUNITY
What is it?

Approaching the moment with gratitude for the opportunity, not overwhelming desire for an external result.

Why does it work?

It releases your mind from the unfair and paralyzing desire for attaining a result you can't actually control – something external – replacing this undermining desire with a positive and productive emotion: Gratitude. This mental shift produces a cool, confident, calm and collected demeanor. The funny part? This demeanor is more likely to actually receive the external result, and more emotionally resilient to not receiving it.

―――

How do you do it?

Repeat the following affirmations to solidify this thought pattern: "I'm just thankful for the opportunity to get [insert result], and while it's certainly desirable, I'm already satisfied by the opportunity to hone my communication skills, regardless of whether or not they produce [insert result]."

10.5: ACCEPT MISTAKES

What is it?

Accepting your stutters, stumbles, and mistakes.

Why does it work?

Dale Carnegie once said, "there are always three speeches, for every one you actually gave. The one you practiced, the one you gave, and the one you wish you gave." You will make mistakes. You will stutter. You will present ideas in suboptimal ways. You will stumble over words. What makes a good speaker? Not someone who doesn't make mistakes. Such a person doesn't exist. Instead, a good speaker reacts to mistakes appropriately, moving on smoothly as if they didn't happen. And the

―――

only way to do this is to accept mistakes, not mentally kick yourself for them.

How do you do it?

Remember this quote, apparently attributed to Winston Churchill (though some dispute this): "When you're 20, you care what everyone thinks, when you're 40 you stop caring what everyone thinks, when you're 60, you realize no one was ever thinking about you in the first place." It's true. Everyone is thinking, "me, me, me" constantly. This doesn't change when you start speaking. And it certainly doesn't change when you make a mistake. Because, chances are, they didn't even realize.

10.6: PERFORM THE "CBT" PROCESS
What is it?

"CBT" stands for cognitive behavioral therapy: Identifying destructive thought patterns and replacing them with positive and productive ones.

Why does it work?

Everyone has self-destructive thoughts. Most people struggle with communication because they have self-destructive thought patterns undermining their confidence. This process removes them.

How do you do it?

First, listen to your internal mental dialogue. Then, notice a self-destructive thought. Next, explain to yourself why it isn't true, and identify the positive thought with which to replace it. Every time this negative thought repeats itself, reiterate the explanation of its falsity and restate the superior thought you want to substitute. Over time, this will condition your mind, sculpting away the negative thoughts undermining your confidence and, as a result, your communication.

10.7: FOCUS EXTERNALLY

What is it?

A hyper-focus on the external situation around you.

___

Why does it work?

It helps overcome self-consciousness: An excessive inward focus creating an overwhelming awareness of self. And it supplies your subconscious mind with inputs to act on, giving it the information it needs to serve up the best possible response on a milli-second by milli-second timeframe.

How do you do it?

There are countless ways. One of the most powerful? A hyper-focus on people's facial expressions. As you know, we have mirror-neurons in our minds. They simulate the feeling of an action, neurologically mirroring what your eyes see. This is how your subconscious mind reads micro-expressions. You say something; you see a tiny shift in someone's expression as a response; your mirror neurons simulate the feeling of making the same shift yourself; and you feel the emotion associated with the shift. And then you can respond to those emotions. This isn't a full-proof, 100% accurate sort of situation. But it's quite close.

___

10.8: FORGET YOURSELF

What is it?

Avoiding hyper self-awareness.

Why does it work?

Most people, when communicating, shift to an excessive focus on themselves. They pay attention to everything about themselves: The sound of their voice, how their words just came out, how they look, how they stand… everything. And yes: You want to ensure you're communicating well. So yes: You want to focus on communicating with the proper techniques. But you don't want to focus on yourself any more than you need to ensure you use the techniques in this book.

How do you do it?

If you direct your focus externally, you won't be able to direct it internally. This is the simple strategy to preventing hyper-self-awareness which morphs into suffocating self-consciousness.

10.9: VISUALIZE SUCCESS

What is it?

Visualize communicating well. Let this visualization carry you away. Live in it.

Why does it work?

Your subconscious mind can't distinguish between a vivid imagination of an experience and the experience itself. And when you visualize speaking successfully, your subconscious mind eventually accepts the premise: *I've spoken successfully.* And when you actually begin to speak, it feels like you've already spoken well and succeeded. Thus, it produces a tremendous amount of confidence.

How do you do it?

It's simple: Imagine it. Don't interrupt the visualization. Engage other senses too, not just sight. And focus on replicating the emotions you would feel. Bring miniscule, specific details to life. And don't imagine externals you can't actually control. Imagine doing the best with what you can control: Your own actions and conduct.

10.10: FOCUS ON WHAT YOU CONTROL
What is it?

Focusing your ambitions on what you can control, and only striving to bring about what you can actually bring about: The proper actions, not any external result.

Why does it work?

Speakers struggle because they feel anxious when they communicate. Anxiety stems from setting as their primary goal an external variable they can't control: A certain response from the audience or a particular outcome. It creates uncertainty. The uncertainty creates fear: Fear of the emotional struggle in the wake of not fulfilling the external goal. Focusing on what you can control avoids this self-destructive dynamic.

How do you do it?

Tell yourself: "All I want to do is perform to the best of my ability. All I want to do is offer the best communication I can produce, practicing the skills I learned. And if I can do this, I will be satisfied." This removes the source of the anxiety, unleashing two

---

incredibly positive things: Confidence (which makes the external result more likely to occur) and peace (if it doesn't).

CONCLUSION

Thank you for trusting me and reading this book. Thank you for giving me the cherished gift of communicating these ideas to you. Thank you for making it possible for me to write about the subject I love for a living.

I hope we have connected through these pages. And I am filled with gratitude, because to me, we have.

I hope these pages served you and helped you accomplish one of the most worthwhile goals: Becoming an infinitely more effective leader by discovering the ten proven steps for mastering communication.

I hope you trust me when I tell you that there is no final destination; there is no stopping point, only constant improvement. You must practice this critical skill of communication every single day, because it is a gift to mankind.

—

We have a special, sacred, unique gift – the gift of spoken word, of connection through airwaves – and we must use it. We must not let it rust away and whither, but exercise it day in and day out.

Through this gift, we can stop or start any mass movement that ripples throughout history long after we leave this Earth.

Through this gift, we can chart a course for our lives and follow it with renewed vigor and greater potential.

Through this gift, we can make the most of this life we've been given and help others do the same.

Through this gift, we can inundate the minds of our fellow humans with ideas that are bold, brave, valuable, and viciously worthwhile; we can break through the barrier that stands between what we want and what we have, by forming big, valiant coalitions of the convinced.

—

———

It is not a question of *if* you will speak, or even of *when*, but of *how*. Will you wield a polished, poised, and precise tool, or one that is dead, degraded, and dulled from the disgrace of disuse?

Will your words be believed, or tossed aside?

Alive with potential, or dead on arrival?

Heeded, or ignored?

Credible, or incredible?

If I've accomplished my goal, you didn't have to think about those questions before you knew the answers. Thank you for letting me try. I hope I've succeeded, just as I hope that you will.

Sincerely, Peter – your partner in striving for success, for the love of the journey, not the destination.

———

___

BONUS ONE
197 HUMAN DESIRES AND HUMAN NEEDS

___

FRAMEWORK #1: THE LIFE-FORCE 8

Evolution creates these. It's that simple. Humans who have acquired the genes (through mutation) that create these desires were more likely to survive and pass them forward. Thus, these "life-force eight" desires are incredibly powerful. They literally keep us alive, and we have genes that force these desires into our minds. In other words: if one of these desires is not met, our brains are screaming at us to "fix it now."

Desire #1: Survival, enjoyment of life, life extension
Desire #2: Enjoyment of food and beverages
Desire #3: Freedom from fear, pain, and danger
Desire #4: Sexual companionship
Desire #5: Comfortable living conditions
Desire #6: To be superior, winning, keeping up
Desire #7: Care and protection of loved ones
Desire #8: Social approval

FRAMEWORK #2: THE LEARNED 9

We've progressed as a society, so for most people, the eight life-force desires are fulfilled. But out of those

---

desires arise the nine learned desires. In other words: we've learned over time that satisfying these desires will end up satisfying our basic human needs: the life-force eight. Cool, right?

Desire #9: To be informed
Desire #10: To satisfy curiosity
Desire #11: Cleanliness of body and surroundings
Desire #12: Efficiency
Desire #13: Convenience
Desire #14: Dependability and quality
Desire #15: Expression of beauty and style
Desire #16: Economy and profit
Desire #17: Bargains

FRAMEWORK #3: THE 6 CORE HUMAN DRIVES

These core human drives are what we do to satisfy our basic human needs and human desires. And think about it: these drives are forces so motivating that they are, in a way, basic human desires on their own. We are so driven to do these things that we *need* them, and thus, you can use them as human desires.

———

Desire #18: Drive to Acquire: the desire to collect material and immaterial things, like a car, or influence

Desire #19: Drive to Bond: the desire to be loved and feel valued in our relationships with others

Desire #20: Drive to Learn: the desire to satisfy our curiosity

Desire #21: Drive to Defend: the desire to protect ourselves, our loved ones and our property

Desire #22: Drive to Feel: the desire for emotional experiences like pleasure or excitement

Desire #23: Drive to Improve: the desire to fulfill our potential and actualize our ambitions

FRAMEWORK #4: MASLOW'S HIERARCHY OF NEEDS

These were advanced by Dr. Abraham Maslow, a famous psychologist who pioneered groundbreaking research into the human condition. These basic human needs, like the life-force eight, come from evolution. And they are arranged in a pyramid, in a hierarchy. Use the hierarchy model to identify what level your audience is on, so you can match your message to it. Here's how this model works: the needs are specifically arranged in

———

a pyramid. And you can't achieve the upper needs unless you fulfill the needs before it. In other words: if someone's physiological needs are not met (no food, warmth, or water), they likely aren't thinking about self-actualizing their fullest potential. So, what you have to do when using this model to tap into your audience's minds, is this: meet them at the level of the hierarchy they are on.

Desire #24: Physiological needs: food, warmth, water, rest
Desire #25: Safety needs: security, safety
Desire #26: Belongingness and love needs: intimate relationships, friends
Desire #27: Esteem needs: prestige and feelings of accomplishment
Desire #28: Self-actualization needs: achieving one's full potential, including creative activities

FRAMEWORK #5: 16-NEED THEORY
"This is a theory of motivation proposed by Steven Reiss, Psychology and Psychiatry professor emeritus at the Ohio State University in Ohio, USA. The concept for this theory originated from the time when Reiss was

hospitalized during the 90s. As he was being treated in the hospital, he was able to observe the devotion and hard work of the nurses who took care of him. As he saw how the nurses loved their work, he began to ask himself questions about what gives happiness to a person." *(https://explorable.com/16-basic-desires-theory)*

Desire #29: Acceptance, the need to be appreciated
Desire #30: Curiosity, the need to gain knowledge
Desire #31: Eating, the need for food
Desire #32: Family, the need to take care of one's offspring
Desire #33: Honor, the need to be faithful to the customary values of an individual's ethnic group, family or clan
Desire #34: Idealism, the need for social justice
Desire #35: Independence, the need to be distinct and self-reliant
Desire #36: Order, the need for prepared, established, and conventional environments that are predictable, safe, and free from random, destructive events
Desire #37: Physical activity, the need for workout of the body
Desire #38: Power, the need for control of will
Desire #39: Romance, the need for mating or sex
Desire #40: Saving, the need to accumulate something

Desire #41: Social contact, the need for relationship with others

Desire #42: Social status, the need for social significance

Desire #43: Tranquility, the need to be secure and protected

Desire #44: Vengeance, the need to strike back against another person

FRAMEWORK #6: ERG THEORY

These come from Maslow's Hierarchy of Needs. "Wait, what?" you ask. Yes. They build upon Maslow's Hierarchy of Needs, by organizing Maslow's basic human needs into "existence," "relatedness," and "growth" buckets. However, each of these three can be treated as a basic human need on their own.

Desire #45: Existence, I want to exist

Desire #46: Relatedness, after I can exist, I want to relate

Desire #47: Growth, after I exist and relate, I want to grow

FRAMEWORK #7: SPIRITUAL NEEDS

It's a grand mystery where the spiritual needs come from. And I'm not going to come up with some explanation that teeters precariously on the line between fact and fiction. Instead, I'll tell you how I've compiled this list. Reading spiritual works. Reading philosophical works. Reading religious works. Reading psychological works. Analyzing the world's most powerful speeches. Analyzing the world's most effective political messages. Analyzing the world's most moving marketing messages. Listening to the wisdom of spiritual leaders. Listening to other people. Listening to myself. Another important way is this: splitting up what others have identified as human needs into sub-needs. For example, transformation splits into empowerment and vision. And also, this: rigorous study of history. If at completely different times of history, in completely different places, completely different civilizations have done the same things, and these things don't seem to satisfy any life-force eight desire, we can use that as a clue to identify spiritual desires.

Desire #48: Ultimate self-realization or acceptance, becoming who you want to be, or wanting to be who you are
Desire #49: The need to reach our potential, doing the most we can possibly do before we die

---

Desire #50: Inspiration, the feeling of spontaneous deep insight, motivating emotions, or creative action

Desire #51: External acceptance, being accepted by others, particularly those we look up to or respect

Desire #52: Transcendence, becoming a part of, or contributing to something larger than yourself

Desire #53: Transformation, transforming into someone better

Desire #54: Wholeness, seeing the affairs of the world, and also personal affairs, become complete

Desire #55: Definition, a simple but strong definition of yourself that tells you who you are

Desire #56: Morals, a set of beliefs about morality, a set of wrongs and rights that guide you

Desire #57: Values, a set of usually immaterial attainments held supreme above all others, that you seek to achieve

Desire #58: Beliefs, a set of beliefs about the world and the way things work that we treat as true

Desire #59: Antitheticals, someone or something different than yourself, to gain self-identity through contrast

Desire #60: Competence, the ability to excel in one or more areas of achievement

---

Desire #61: Freedom, the feeling of being able to go where you want, think what you want, say what you want, and do what you want

Desire #62: Hope, the desire to expect and believe in something that hasn't yet happened, particularly the freedom from negative experiences

Desire #63: Identity association, the desire to associate with a group, tribe, or team rallied around a common identity

Desire #64: External completeness, the desire to attain something outside of yourself that will make you complete

Desire #65: Understanding, the desire to be understood by other people

Desire #66: Life after death, the desire to exist, in some form, after your body dies

Desire #67: External peace, the desire to live in tranquility, with stability and calm

Desire #68: Internal acceptance, being accepted by oneself

Desire #69: Legacy, leaving something behind that exists after you died, or being eternally remembered for something

Desire #70: Knowing, the desire to discover new truths

Desire #71: Truth, the desire to separate what is true from what is false

---

Desire #72: Internal peace, the desire to have inner tranquility

Desire #73: Explanation, a way to explain the human experience

Desire #74: God, the desire to identify and reach a higher being

Desire #75: Meaning, the desire to discover a purpose in life

Desire #76: Vision, the desire to subscribe and work towards a specific vision of the future

Desire #77: Generosity, the innate desire we have to be generous to our fellow humans materially and immaterially

Desire #78: Difference, the desire to be different, the desire to not be average, the desire to be more than average

Desire #79: Heard, the desire to be heard, the desire to communicate

Desire #80: Nostalgia, the desire to return to a time long gone, which is fondly remembered

Desire #81: Connection, the desire to feel like you are connected to people, places, and things

Desire #82: Virtue, the desire to fit your conception of "good"

Desire #83: Clarity, freedom from confusion about salient matters

Desire #84: Alignment, freedom from cognitive dissonance (holding two conflicting pieces of information in mind at once, and the discomfort this produces), alignment between someone's idea of themselves and reality

———

FRAMEWORK #8: ECONOMIC DESIRES

These are how people separate the good products from the bad ones. And know this: when I say product, that doesn't only mean a physical product. Ideas are products. Plans are products. Suggestions to your boss at work are products. Many of these economic desires apply not only to physical products but to that expanded definition of a product. If these economic human desires are not met, a person probably won't buy a product. Luckily for you, you'll know exactly what they are and how to express them for easy persuasive communication.

Desire #85: Efficacy, how well does it work?

Desire #86: Comparative efficacy, how well does it stack up?

Desire #87: Speed, how quickly does it work?

Desire #88: Reliability, can I depend on it to do what I want?

Desire #89: Comparative reliability, is it more dependable than all other options?

Desire #90: Product-problem fit, does this solve my particular problem?

Desire #91: Ease of use, how much effort does it require?

———

_____

Desire #92: Comparative ease of use, is there an easier option?

Desire #93: Flexibility, how many things does it do?

Desire #94: Comparative flexibility, does another option do more things than this option?

Desire #95: Status, how does this affect the way others perceive me?

Desire #96: Aesthetic appeal, how attractive or otherwise aesthetically pleasing is it?

Desire #97: Emotion, how does it make me feel?

Desire #98: Cost, how much do I have to give up to get this?

Desire #99: Comparative cost, is it a good deal?

FRAMEWORK #9: ROBBIN'S 6 NEEDS

Tony Robbins, success coach and motivational speaker (amongst many other impressive pursuits) has identified these as the core motivating desires of the people he has met. The first four needs are defined as needs of the personality, and the last two are identified as needs of the spirit.

Desire #100: Certainty, assurance you can avoid pain and gain pleasure

_____

——

Desire #101: Uncertainty and variety, the need for the unknown, change, new stimuli

Desire #102: Significance, feeling unique, important, special or needed

Desire #103: Connection and love, a strong feeling of closeness or union with someone or something

Desire #104: Growth, an expansion of capacity, capability or understanding

Desire #105: Contribution, a sense of service and focus on helping, giving to and supporting others

FRAMEWORK #10: RUSSEL'S CORE 4

These come from Bertrand Russel's Nobel Prize acceptance speech. Let me quote him: "All human activity is prompted by desire. There is a wholly fallacious theory advanced by some earnest moralists to the effect that it is possible to resist desire in the interests of duty and moral principle. I say this is fallacious, not because no man ever acts from a sense of duty, but because duty has no hold on him unless he desires to be dutiful. If you wish to know what men will do, you must know not only, or principally, their material

——

———

circumstances, but rather the whole system of their desires with their relative strengths."

Desire #106: Acquisitiveness, "the wish to possess as much as possible of goods, or the title to goods"

Desire #107: Rivalry, "a great many men will cheerfully face impoverishment if they can thereby secure complete ruin for their rivals, hence the present level of taxation"

Desire #108: Vanity, "[It] is one of the most fundamental desires of the human heart. It can take innumerable forms, from buffoonery to the pursuit of posthumous fame"

Desire #109: Love of Power, "Many people prefer glory to power, but on the whole these people have less effect upon the course of events than those who prefer power to glory: power, like vanity, is insatiable"

FRAMEWORK #11: FEAR NEEDS

These are all desires based in the freedom from some fear. The fears that keep us up at night, and that torment us daily, are all part of these basic human desires. In other words: these are all desires that are the *absence* of something we fear. You'll see what I mean.

———

———

Desire #110: Freedom from loss

Desire #111: Freedom from danger

Desire #112: Freedom from being left out

Desire #113: Freedom from criticism

Desire #114: Freedom from bad decisions

Desire #115: Freedom from disappointing others

Desire #116: Freedom from loss of autonomy

Desire #117: Freedom from separation

Desire #118: Freedom from ego-death

Desire #119: Freedom from fear

Desire #120: Freedom from guilt

Desire #121: Freedom from [insert harm]

Desire #122: Relief

Desire #123: Escape

FRAMEWORK #12: HUMAN DESIRES OF THE MODERN ERA

These desires are new. Did we always want "more time?" Not as much as we wanted to hunt for our next meal, so we didn't die. But since we're now far removed from our natural state of chasing our base desires (the life-force

———

———

eight), we have new desires. Now we would all love more time to do things we love.

.

Desire #124: Happiness, people want to achieve some abstract, personal definition of happiness

Desire #125: Conserving financial resources, people want to be free from the guilt of spending money

Desire #126: Conserving time, people want to avoid wasting their limited time

Desire #127: Building social networks, people want to enlarge their social networks and use them for fulfillment

Desire #128: Gaining status, people want to rise to positions of status, specifically in their existing social structures

Desire #129: Accumulating resources, people want to gather as many resources as possible, they want to "collect"

Desire #130: The desire for meaning, people want to identify a meaning, a reason for living, to escape the insane absurdity of not having a reason to live

Desire #131: Winning power and position, and controlling others

Desire #132: Access, people want access to exclusive people, places, and events

Desire #133: Scarcity, people want what there is not a lot of

———

Desire #134: Loss aversion, people want to avoid loss more than they want to experience gain

Desire #135: Premium, people want to have a step above average in all aspects of life

Desire #136: Symbolism, people want to attach symbols of status and success to their lives

Desire #137: Reduced anxiety, people want to feel relaxed and escape anxiety

Desire #138: Reduced workload, people want to work less and play more

Desire #139: More time, people want to fill less of their time with involuntary activity

Desire #140: Adequacy, people want to feel like they are enough and don't need to change

Desire #141: Esteem, people want to feel loved by others

Desire #142: Liberation, people want to feel liberated from the lasting traumas of their pasts

Desire #143: Respect, self-respect, and respect from others

Desire #144: Confidence, people want to believe in themselves

Desire #145: Inclusion, people want to be included

Desire #146: Distraction, people want to be distracted from their larger problems

---

Desire #147: Intellectualism, people want to work in an intellectually stimulating environment

FRAMEWORK #13: WEAKNESS NEEDS

These come from our weakest impulses. You'll see what I mean. They are impulses we would be embarrassed to admit we have. But, undeniably, almost every single human being has at least one of these. Probably more.

Desire #148: Accommodating past failures, living in a way molded around preventing the trauma of past failures from reoccurring

Desire #149: Association, forming a network of associative relationships to people, ideas, beliefs, and tribes

Desire #150: Simplicity, the desire to escape complexity and interact with simple situations instead

Desire #151: Guidance, being assisted by an expert who will help you achieve success

Desire #152: Ease, living without hardship

Desire #153: Victimization, the excuse to blame other people, events, or institutions for one's problems to avoid taking personal responsibility for them

---

Desire #154: Meeting expectations, the desire to meet the expectations others have of us, instead of what we want

Desire #155: Approval, the desire to receive approval from others, even if we don't approve of them ourselves

Desire #156: Fear of rejection, the desire to escape rejection

Desire #157: Validation, the desire to have our actions and beliefs proven valid by others

Desire #158: Fitting in, the desire to exist as a defined member of a supportive group

Desire #159: Attention, the desire to receive attention from others

Desire #160: Reciprocation, the desire for others to reciprocate the way we feel about them

FRAMEWORK #14: EVIL DESIRES

These desires are tribal. They are primitive. They are primal. They are engineered into us by evolution. They stem from the influence of the negative-ego. Freud would have called it the "id." Much of what goes wrong in the world is the product of these desires.

Desire #161: Revenge, the desire to strike back against someone or something which hurt us

---

———

Desire #162: Superiority, the desire to be superior to other people

Desire #163: Competition, the desire to compete and win for the satisfaction of ego demands

Desire #164: Judgement, the desire to pass judgment onto others

Desire #165: Suffering of others, the desire to not suffer while others are

Desire #166: Status, prestige, elitism, the desire to belong to a separate and superior class

Desire #167: Aggression, the desire to attack others, typically non-physically

Desire #168: Greed, the desire to amass more than we could ever possibly need

Desire #169: Power, the desire to control the lives of others

Desire #170: Importance, the desire to be important

Desire #171: Ego satisfaction, the desire to meet the demands of our negative ego

FRAMEWORK #15: ESTEEM NEEDS

They were first identified in Maslow's Hierarchy of Needs. But they can be broken down much further. We see them in people who seem to be "living for others."

———

They do what others want them to, seeking to gain esteem.

Desire #172: Admiration, being praised by others
Desire #173: Popularity, being liked by large amounts of others
Desire #174: Desired, being wanted both socially and romantically
Desire #175: Ownership, feeling ownership over things that can't actually be owned
Desire #176: Possession, wanting to satisfy possessive impulses
Desire #177: Being envied, wanting others to be jealous of you

FRAMEWORK #16: PRIMAL HUMAN NEEDS

These are wired so deep into our minds. Why? Because thousands of years ago, they helped us survive. People who had the gene that created these desires were more likely to survive and pass those genes onto their offspring. We see them in the common actions we all take. Why do we work? Why do we try to earn money? Why do we exercise? The answers seem obvious. But we do it to satisfy our primal, basic human needs, and human desires.

___

Desire #178: Survival, the desire to extend life.

Desire #179: Primitive desire to be safe, the desire to live away from all threats

Desire #180: Primitive desire to be healthy, the desire to have a healthy body

Desire #181: Strength, the desire to have a physically strong body

Desire #182: Resources, enough economic and social resources to eat

Desire #183: Drink, the desire to drink

Desire #184: Reproduce, the desire to pass on our genetic material to offspring

Desire #185: Fend off foes, the desire to protect ourselves from other people who threaten us

Desire #186: Providing, the desire to provide for our offspring

Desire #187: Fighting, the desire to physically engage others

FRAMEWORK #17: MY 7P MODEL

After researching this subject for a long, long time, and diving deep into the dark depths of the human desires and human needs, I've come up with this model. It is, in

___

———

part, a particular categorization of the other identified needs.

Desire #188: People, we desire meaningful relationships with people.

Desire #189: Purpose, we desire a defined purpose.

Desire #190: Progress, we desire to progress towards our defined purpose.

Desire #191: Plan, we desire a plan for achieving our purpose.

Desire #192: Protection, we desire to protect ourselves and our property.

Desire #193: Property, we desire to gain more property.

Desire #194: Passion, we desire to center our lives around a main activity we are passionate about.

In other words: people want to progress towards a purpose they are passionate about with the right people and a plan, and they want to protect their property and get new property.

BONUS TWO
25 COGNITIVE BIASES

.

BIAS #1: REWARD-PUNISHMENT TENDENCY
What is it?
We adopt behaviors benefiting us, protecting us from harm, or both.

Where does it come from?
Human life is choosing between behaviors and experiencing a benefit or punishment as a result of the choice. Due to the inherent, inalienable, intrinsic nature of our existence in this universe, we evolved to seek benefits in all situations, and avoid losses in all situations. Of the two, the threat of a loss is more motivating. Why? We feel the pain of loss more than the pleasure of an equivalent gain, sometimes twice as much. Loss-aversion strikes again.

BIAS #2: LIKING-LOVING TENDENCY
What is it?
We find people we like or love more persuasive, and we ignore their flaws and faults.

Where does it come from?

We are social creatures who evolved in the presence of our fellow humans. This psychological tendency emerged because it conferred an evolutionary advantage (which helps us survive and thus pass on our genes containing the tendency). What's the advantage? Stronger human relationships protecting us in urgent moments.

BIAS #3: DISLIKING-HATING TENDENCY
What is it?

We find people we hate less persuasive, while amplifying their faults and ignoring their positive qualities.

Where does it come from?

This is a possible explanation, and one not scientifically validated. It's just my hypothesis. The disliking and hating tendency evolved because it activates the liking and loving tendency, which helps us survive by forming stronger human bonds. The disliking and hating tendency offers no advantage on its own. But it activates something that does. How can hating someone make us

---

———

love someone? The explanation is this: You hate person X, you hear person Y hates person X too, and now you and person Y are best buddies. In other words, the disliking and hating tendency strengthens group bonds unified around hatred, which can help members of the in-group survive. Why? Because they have stronger bonds through the liking and loving tendency with other members of the in-group. We've seen historical disasters stemming from this time and time again. The *short-term* beneficiaries? Members of the in-group.

BIAS #4: DOUBT AVOIDANCE TENDENCY
What is it?
We tend to avoid doubt. We tune-out opposing information, gravitate towards unambiguous "truths," arbitrarily select sources of "truth," and prematurely leap to a conclusion to escape doubt, where we remain entrenched no matter what we hear.

Where does it come from? This stems from our tendency to conserve cognitive resources. Why did we evolve to conserve cognitive resources? In the dire

———

straits of a life-threatening situation, we need our minds to be agile and active, not sluggish from the strain of unimportant decisions. In fact, all biases stem, in part, from our tendency to conserve cognitive resources. Why? They're all shortcuts.

BIAS #5: INCONSISTENCY AVOIDANCE TENDENCY
What is it?
People tend to avoid acting inconsistently with past actions.

Where does it come from?
Our innate human desire to limit confusion and conserve cognitive resources by organizing the world in artificially neat ways, in which we always acted correctly (thus there's no need to be inconsistent with our past selves). We also conserve mental resources by saying "I probably thought this action through the first time, so this time, I'll trust my past-self."

———

BIAS #6: CURIOSITIY TENDENCY
What is it?

We want to *know*, particularly if we know there's something we don't know. For example, you're more curious if I say "there are ___ tons of bananas on Earth," than if I never said anything about Earth's aggregate banana tonnage.

Where does it come from?

Evolution. Noticing a pattern here? Funny: We also evolved to notice patterns. Why? Once again, to conserve mental resources. But how is it evolutionary? Knowing more, a function of a curious mind, helps us survive and pass on our genetic material. Thus, the genes creating curiosity survive.

BIAS #7: KANTIAN FAIRNESS TENDENCY
What is it?

We tend to believe the world ought to be fair, treat others how we want to be treated, and get extremely, irrationally offended when someone breaches fairness.

———

Where does it come from?

Anything that fosters positive relationships between humans helps us survive. The genes containing survival-boosting traits or tendencies, because we survive and reproduce when we have these tendencies, get passed on.

BIAS #8: ENVY AND JEALOUSY TENDENCY
What is it?

We hate seeing possessions or achievements we want for ourselves in the clutches of others.

Where does it come from?

Our inherent need to compete for limited resources, and our attempts to satisfy our unlimited demands with a finite resource-pool.

BIAS #9: RECIPROCATION TENDENCY
What is it?

We seek to reciprocate behaviors, positive or negative.

___

Where does it come from?

Evolution. Much like the loving and liking tendency, it fosters stronger human bonds. And it yields punishment in the form of negative reciprocation when those bonds are betrayed, disincentivizing betrayal.

BIAS #10: MERE ASSOCIATION INFLUENCE
What is it?

When we see a new item clumped in a group of good items, we believe it is also good. When we see a new item clumped in a group of bad items, we assume it is also bad. In short: We identify the traits of a new item by extrapolating from its surroundings.

Where does it come from?

Our need to conserve cognitive resources.

BIAS #11: PAIN-AVOIDING PSYCHOLOGICAL DENIAL
What is it?

We habitually ignore or deny psychologically painful information until it's bearable.

___

―

Where does it come from?

Our evolutionary need to maintain an active and agile mind, unbridled by draining concerns.

BIAS #12: EXCESSIVE SELF-REGARD TENDENCY
What is it?

We all think we are above average.

Where does it come from?

Confidence is self-fulfilling. 2,000 years ago, if you overconfidently believed you could survive a mammoth hunt, self-belief helped you survive. Thus, you passed down the genes. Likewise, humans have a biological tendency to fight (physically and otherwise) only if they perceive their opponent is unwilling to fight back. Excessive self-regard tendency makes us willing to fight. So we avoid a fight in the first place, survive, and pass down excessive self-regard tendency.

BIAS #13: OVER-OPTIMISM TENDENCY
What is it?

Excess optimism is the normal human condition.

Where does it come from?

It helps us conserve mental resources. It ties to many cognitive biases and mental heuristics. It lightens the burden of life on a difficult planet.

BIAS #14: DEPRIVAL SUPERREACTION TENDENCY

What is it?

Loss-aversion. We prefer to avoid pains more than reap rewards. Sometimes twice as much. -$1,000 can be twice as painful as +$1,000 is pleasurable. And once we lose something, we react with overwhelming intensity – irrational intensity – in trying to restore the loss. We also tend to place an irrational amount of effort in pursuing a goal we just *barely* missed.

Where does it come from?

2,000 years ago, behaviors tied to protecting what we had – territory, resources, food, members of our tribe – probably helped us survive more than striving to get more. Thus, we are evolutionarily and genetically coded to avoid loss and play the game of life conservatively.

BIAS #15: SOCIAL-PROOF TENDENCY
What is it?

We follow the crowd and look to others for direction.

Where does it come from?

We have two salient evolutionary needs genetically coding this tendency. We need to conserve mental resources and we need the protection offered by a tribe. Social proof conserves mental resources because instead of using mental calories to make our own decisions, we outsource our judgement to the crowd. Secondly, it helps us maintain "group-member status" because aligning our actions with the crowd permits us into the crowd.

BIAS #16: CONTRAST-MISREACTION TENDENCY
What is it?

We judge items not on their inherent qualities, but on how they compare to points of reference.

Where does it come from?

This is a side-effect of our cognitive machinery. It can cause silly and frequent misjudgments. We can't judge anything on its own, unless we have a point of comparison. We're happy with our $60,000 salary until we find out our coworker makes $62,000. But $60,000 equals $60,000, no matter what anyone else makes. Sadly, that's not how our judgement works. We always use points of comparison to reach conclusions.

BIAS #17: STRESS-MISINFLUENCE TENDENCY

What is it?

We make premature, extreme, and irrationally quick decisions under high stress.

Where does it come from?

2,000 years ago, when a saber-tooth tiger jumped in front of us, creating high cognitive stress, we needed to make a quick decision: Run, or fight? (Probably run: It has "saber-tooth" in its name...) In this situation, a part of the brain called the amygdala turns on. It shuts down the prefrontal cortex, which performs slow, methodical,

---

---

deliberate logical operations. The problem? The amygdala turns on and suppresses logic even if we need logic to solve the source of the stress; even if it's a sales pitch or an interview (logic-demanding), not a saber-tooth tiger (agility-demanding).

BIAS #18: AVAILABILITY MIS-WEIGHING TENDENCY
What is it?
We overweigh evidence that comes quickly to mind.

Where does it come from?
Conservation of mental resources. It's a mental short-cut that is a rough, approximate, "good enough" judgement in most cases. In other cases? It produces serious misjudgments.

BIAS #19: USE IT OR LOSE IT TENDENCY
What is it?
We lose stored information if we don't use it.

———

Where does it come from?

To conserve our finite budget of mental resources, we gradually dump information we don't use.

BIAS #20: DRUG MISINFLUENCE TENDENCY
What is it?

Drugs cause poor cognition.

Where does it come from?

Drugs. How do you use it in communication? I'm legally compelled to say this: Don't drug your audience. Truth be told, there's not much you can do to activate this tendency in an ethical way. Offering coffee works. Maybe some alcoholic beverages, when appropriate, to smooth over an interaction. Coffee might make your audience more attentive, and give them a dopamine hit. The happier people are, the more open they are to persuasive appeals. It also activates reciprocity, likeability, and related biases. I suppose we'll stick with this advice: The only way to ethically activate this one is by offering coffee when it's in your power to do so.

———

———

BIAS #21: SENESCENCE-MISINFLUENCE TENDENCY

What is it?

Older people are prone to more faulty cognition than younger people.

Where does it come from?

Old age.

BIAS #22: AUTHORITY-MISINFLUENCE TENDENCY

What is it?

We find authority figures persuasive.

Where does it come from?

This probably facilitated more fruitful and well-organized tribe- and group-relations, and as a result, helped us survive. It also conserves mental resources. It would strain our cognitive resources to learn the entire medical discipline when we have a sickness. It's more efficient to outsource to an expert.

———

BIAS #23: TWADDLE TENDENCY
What is it?

Spending significant time on useless activities. Procrastinating.

Where does it come from?

Our innate drive to keep cognitive load down. Why procrastinate? Because it's mentally easier. Starting the next task, or taking the next action, taxes our discipline. Our discipline functions like a finite budget: It runs out eventually. After a long day, when we know the next task is mentally straining, we twaddle because it's just easier.

BIAS #24: REASON RESPECTING TENDENCY
What is it?

We respect requests and believe statements justified by reasons.

Where does it come from?

One of the processes we use to conserve cognitive resources is called substitution. We substitute an easy question for a hard one. How does this interact with

---

———

reason-respecting tendency? We substitute the easy question "is there a reason for this?" for the hard question "is this a good and valid reason?" Simply hearing a reason often does the trick, even if it's invalid.

BIAS #25: THE LOLLAPALOOZA TENDENCY
What is it?

Any psychological tendency pushing a particular behavior persuades. Multiple pushing the same behavior persuade exponentially more, resulting in massive persuasive force. Munger calls it a "lollapalooza effect." It happens when multiple cognitive biases converge all at once, in the same direction.

Where does it come from?

It comes from the individual influence of each bias. Combined, their persuasion is more than their sum. It is a case of one plus one equals three.

———

.

Made in the USA
Las Vegas, NV
26 May 2021